D0973123

CHATEAUBRIAND

Atala

René

A New Translation by IRVING PUTTER

Berkeley, Los Angeles, London
UNIVERSITY OF CALIFORNIA PRESS

UNIVERSITY OF CALIFORNIA PRESS
BERKELEY AND LOS ANGELES, CALIFORNIA
UNIVERSITY OF CALIFORNIA PRESS, LTD.
LONDON, ENGLAND
COPYRIGHT, 1952, BY THE
REGENTS OF THE UNIVERSITY OF CALIFORNIA
SEVENTH PRINTING, 1973
ISBN: 0-520-00223-7
PRINTED IN THE UNITED STATES OF AMERICA

TO THE MEMORY
OF MY PARENTS

INTRODUCTION

Few books in France have met with the success which greeted *Atala* in 1801. Within a year of its publication it boasted five French editions, and its success spread rapidly abroad as Spanish, Italian, German, and English translations appeared in quick succession. Overnight Chateaubriand was catapulted from obscurity to the heights of the literary firmament, where he remained for the rest of his life as a star of the first magnitude. It was hardly necessary to read the book to know about Atala, her lover, and Father Aubry; their waxen images stood like little saints in the stalls along the Seine, reproductions hung in the inns, their likenesses were used to adorn brass clocks or dinnerware, and the characters were represented on the stage.

What qualities could the book have to attract such enthusiasm? Probably no simple answer would suffice, but one fact stands out: *Atala*—and *The Genius of Christianity,* which was published the following year—could not have appeared at a more opportune moment in French history.

After the violent decade of the 1790's France could look back on a long period of glory and suffering. She had spread her intellectual and political hegemony over most of Europe in the seventeenth century, and she could not forget the brilliant heritage of Louis XIV, Racine, and Bossuet. In the following century—the century of Voltaire, Diderot, and Rousseau—men sought passionately, in an atmosphere of intellectual ferment, for new answers to age-old philosophical and social problems. What is man's place in the cosmos? How must we view God? Is civilization a blessing or a curse? All these questions are echoed in *Atala.*

The eighteenth century had largely been the century of the search for truth. Reason and analysis were the order of the day. Man as a rational being and man's social behavior were explored. Religion was undermined, and Christianity attacked as ridiculous in its beliefs, cruel in its methods, and an enemy of culture. Nature was virtually ignored. The scintillating and incisive style of Voltaire, bare of emotional appeal, was the proper vehicle for such a society.

The reaction came as the century wore on. New values were sought that would satisfy not the intellect, but the heart. Rousseau saw the divine presence in the beauty and harmony of the universe. Frenchmen found a profusion of emotion in English literature—Richardson, Fielding, Gray, Young, and Thomson were avidly read in France in the latter part of the eighteenth century. The mysterious atmosphere of Ossian, which had so fascinated Goethe in his *Werther,* also had its effect on young men growing up in France just before the revolution; its influence is manifest in René's solitary wanderings over the heath. And *Werther* itself, with its portrayal of love related to a quest after the absolute and despair with the human condition, resulting in suicide, produced a profound impression in France. Fifteen translations, adaptations, or editions of *Werther* appeared in France between 1776 and 1797; René's temperament bears many comparisons with the temperament of the young German. Thus Frenchmen sought new experiences in emotion. Tears became fashionable at the theater as dramas grew increasingly melodramatic.

More powerfully than any other writer Rousseau contributed to and influenced this growing concern with feelings. He turned away from the iniquity of man to the consolation of nature's mountains, lakes, and moonlight. France changed its formal cultivated gardens to the English and Chinese type of garden of charming disorder and fantasy. Descriptions of scenery in literature became more brilliant and colorful. The accounts of Cook, Bougainville, Lapeyrouse, and other travelers revealed to a civilized French society the cultures of primitive peoples and the lush settings in which they lived. The "noble savage" close to nature was held to be more virtuous and free than civilized man corrupted by the institutions of his society. Bernardin de Saint-Pierre painted dazzling pictures of tropical seas and virgin forests in his *Studies of Nature* and *Paul and Virginia,* and the success of the latter must have been an incentive to the young Chateaubriand.

These were the currents which set the scene for Francois-René de Chateaubriand. He was born at Saint-Malo, Brittany, on September 4, 1768, the last of ten children, four of whom had died early. Of the survivors the eldest was a male heir and the next four were girls. "My four sisters," writes Chateaubriand in his *Memoirs,* "probably owed their existence to my father's desire to have his name assured by a second son; but I resisted, I had an aversion for life." Thus, like Byron's Cain, the author tells us that he never asked for the present of life; he is in effect formulating one of the fundamental postulates of pessimists through the ages, that it were better for man never to have been born.

He grew up, wandering along the beaches of Saint-Malo, rather neglected by his parents. His dry and despotic father lavished no affection on his children. "His customary manner was a profound sadness which grew deeper with age, and a silence from which he emerged only in fits of anger . . . What was felt in his presence was fear." His mother, naturally gay and affable, was repressed by the disappointments of her life with her husband, and had retired to revery consoled by piety. According to the author, she showed a blind preference for her elder son, while his youngest sister, Lucile, was "the most neglected and the least loved" of the daughters.

Instinctively the two youngest children were drawn to each other, not merely because of their situation in the family, but because of the affinity of their temperaments. Lucile was as sensitive as her brother and shared his moody spells of depression. Like her mother she was passionately stirred by religion. She would accompany her brother on

his walks through the woods, and she it was, says Chateaubriand, who first suggested to him that he "paint" the emotions he felt so strongly. Lucile was to become the model
for Amelia in *René*. To what extent the morbid relation-
ship in the book reflects reality in the life of the young
people we cannot be sure. Lucile was four years older than
her brother. She was married, when she was thirty-two, to
a man almost seventy years old, who left her a widow after
six months of marriage, while she herself died at the age
of forty in a neurotic condition bordering on insanity.
Scipion Marin and Sainte-Beuve insinuate, and Lemaître
takes great pains to insist, that the book relates what really
existed, but there is no compelling reason to believe that
this is so. Chateaubriand himself indignantly denied it, and
others have pointed out that the theme of abnormal affections was far from uncommon in eighteenth-century literature. Incest was also utilized in such works as Goethe's
Wilhelm Meister (1795) and Byron's *Manfred* (1817), and,
of course, it was one of the themes of ancient literature,
which Chateaubriand knew so well. Amelia is not identical
with Lucile any more than René is with the author, but
morally they are undoubtedly the same.

In 1778 the family went to live at their manor house
at Combourg, a forbidding feudal dwelling, where Chateaubriand was to spend his adolescence in solitude until he
was eighteen. Then a lieutenant's commission was obtained
for him.

In the army and in Paris he was initiated into the irre-
ligious atmosphere of prerevolutionary French society. In
1791 he decided to visit America. His motive for this trip
is not clear. Was he serious about his plan of finding the
much-sought Northwest Passage? Or was he more concerned
about finding local color for *The Natchez*, his projected
epic about the man of nature? Or was he simply anxious
to leave revolutionary France? Doubtless all of these entered
into his plans.

He spent five months in America. It is well established

now that Chateaubriand could not in this short period have seen all the country he describes. In fact, it is safe to say that he did not see the Mississippi nor "the Floridas" at all. Probably his acquaintance with America was confined to the territory between Baltimore and the Niagara Falls, and he may well have met some Indians during his stay. But if his experience in the New World was limited, the impressions he received were intense enough to furnish him with rich material for his writings.

He returned to France in 1792. Here he allowed himself to be married in a loveless match, which never interfered with a succession of affairs he had with other women in the following years. Soon afterwards he joined the army of the princes, was wounded by shell fire, and suffered from fever and smallpox. In 1793 he left the Continent and joined the émigrés in London.

For seven years he lived in poverty in England, preparing for his literary career and subsisting on what he could earn as a translator and teacher. The despondency of this exile is reflected in the conclusion of *Atala* and in Atala's song in the wilderness. During this period he published his first work, *Essay on Revolutions* (1797), a pessimistic and often antireligious study.

Soon afterwards a fundamental change in Chateaubriand's beliefs occurred. The revolution had not dealt kindly with his royalist family. His mother and sisters had been imprisoned, and his brother and sister-in-law executed. In the final months of 1798 a letter from one of his sisters announced the death of his mother, and a few months later the sister who had written the letter died also. "These two voices emerging from the tomb . . . struck me," wrote Chateaubriand; "I became a Christian. I was not governed, I confess, by any mighty supernatural insight; my conversion came from the heart; I wept and I believed."

He now conceived the idea of writing a work which would be at once a personal expiation of his faithless past and an apology of Christianity. He began his composition when

he was still in England. In 1800, after Napoleon had con-
solidated his position by his election as consul for ten years,
Chateaubriand considered it safe enough to return to
France. Here he completed *The Genius of Christianity*.
Because, he said, he feared that *Atala* would be pirated, but,
more likely to prepare public opinion for his major work,
he detached the episode of *Atala* and published it separately
in 1801 with the success we have seen. When *The Genius
of Christianity* appeared in 1802 it won the immediate ac-
claim its author had hoped for and became one of the important works of his time. Its publication was perfectly
timed. For twelve years churches in Paris had been closed
and profaned, or had served as club headquarters, stores,
or prisons. In the provinces vandalism was apparent as abandoned churches showed steeples without bells, cemeteries
without crosses, and headless saints. France was ripe for a
religious renaissance. The signal for the revival was given
when Napoleon signed his concordat with the pope on April
18, 1802. Four days earlier Chateaubriand's apology had
made its appearance.

The subtitle to his work, *Poetic and Moral Beauties of
the Christian Religion,* gave the clue to his argument.
Chateaubriand was less interested in proving the truth of
Christianity than in demonstrating its artistic superiority,
the beauty of its ceremonies, and the majesty of its cathe-
drals. According to Chateaubriand, no religion ever penetrated the human heart so deeply, and none is so apt to
inspire works of genius. Thus his book is a poet's argument.
His reasons are addressed to the heart and the senses; beauty
becomes the measure of truth. This, in fact, is the Christianity presented in *René*—a religion of bells and incense.

Of unquestionable weakness as a philosophical work,
The Genius of Christianity nevertheless exerted a powerful
influence because of its eloquence of style and imaginative
qualities. It became a spiritual guide and a manifesto for
the coming romantic movement. For the author himself it
won the favor of Napoleon, who appointed him to two

diplomatic posts, thus beginning his political career. When Napoleon, however, allowed Louis de Bourbon, Duc d'Enghien, to be shot as a traitor after a secret and illegal trial, Chateaubriand resigned in protest. He spent the following years traveling in Mediterranean countries or living in seclusion at his estate at Aulnay. He expressed his opposition to Napoleon in an article in the *Mercure de France* and agitated for the restoration of the Bourbons. Louis XVIII, grateful for a pamphlet that, he declared, had been worth a hundred thousand men to the Bourbon cause, made Chateaubriand minister of the interior in 1815. Now the same man who had once had the courage to protest the injustice done to the Duc d'Enghien became a party, for a time, to the excesses of the royalist reaction, extolling the restored king's "fatherly chastisement," though such chastisement could mean death, as indeed it did for popular Marshal Ney.

The next years saw Chateaubriand as ambassador to Berlin (1821) and London (1822) and as foreign minister (1823). In the latter capacity, despite his liberal tendencies, he engineered the unpopular war of intervention in Spain, restoring the despotic rule of Ferdinand VII and, in effect, supporting the policy of Metternich to gain prestige for France—and himself. After a final appointment as ambassador to Rome (1828), he retired from political life with the fall of the Bourbons in 1830.

His declining years were spent in morose retirement comforted, however, by the attentions of Madame Récamier. Sickness, old age, and inactivity were a constant source of depression. He died July 4, 1848, to the end a self-contradictory character—an interpreter of freedom-loving savages who helped suppress the aspirations of freedom-loving Spaniards, a torch bearer of Christianity who was himself all but a stranger to dogma, an extoller of marriage as the "pivot of social economy" who never let his precepts inhibit his pleasures. He was buried on the little storm-swept island of Grand-Bé off the coast of Brittany.

His chief works, aside from those already mentioned, are *The Martyrs* (1809), an unsuccessful epic depicting the persecution of the Christians by Diocletian in the third century, the *Itinerary from Paris to Jerusalem* (1811), based on the author's trip to the Orient, and, most important of all, his *Memoirs from Beyond the Grave,* written over a period of thirty years and published, according to his own desire, after his death. In the *Memoirs* Chateaubriand tells the dramatic story of his ambitious life, often exaggerating or "editing" the facts to show himself in a favorable light. Talking safely from the grave he now revealed his incapacity for sincere attachments except for Madame Récamier. Nevertheless, despite glaring inconsistencies and a constant display of the author's vanity, the color, variety, and vigor of the *Memoirs* make this work the finest creation of Chateaubriand.

To a considerable extent the success of *The Genius of Christianity* depended on the ethusiasm of the public for its two most striking episodes, *Atala* and *René,* the first included to illustrate the section entitled "Harmonies of Religion with Scenes of Nature and Passions of the Human Heart," and the second to warn of the dangers of solitude and vague passions and to show how religion can heal the wounds caused by them.

Originally, however, *Atala* had been intended as an episode of *The Natchez,* the epic of the man of nature, which appeared belatedly in 1826. Chateaubriand even claims that *Atala* was written "in the cabins of the Indians." To what extent this is true we may only conjecture. Certainly he cannot have written it all in America, at least in its definitive form, for almost to the turn of the century he was a disciple of the anticlerical "philosophes," while *Atala* appeared as part of a call to religion and a denial of the "philosophes." It may have been sketched in America, was probably composed in the main in London, and completed after the author's conversion. Almost inevitably, therefore, the dual and contradictory inspiration reveals itself.

Today we are less moved than the faith-starved public of 1800 by Chateaubriand's attempt to rehabilitate religion. The didactic tone of the religious parts and the self-conscious Biblical references do not enhance the author's art. Certain incidents in the text seem, moreover, to indicate that in their deepest consciousness the Indian lovers are unregenerate. Beneath the religious layer natural man perseveres, and many a phrase uttered by the Indians are echoes of Rousseau.

The characterizations are as heterogeneous as the philosophical tendencies. Chateaubriand has in fact informed his Indian lovers with the ardent romantic temperament of the early nineteenth century. Beyond this they are to a certain extent reflections of the author himself, and their feelings are the product of an old and complex culture, one which has suffered much, reflected on its own nature, and learned to articulate its thought in abstract terminology. Chateaubriand is not a novelist but a poet, and is incapable of creating characters apart from himself.

In his own day this was an advantage. The emotions he expressed were intimately felt and were accepted by his generation as genuine. Today much of this emotion is inevitably dated. After decades of realism and satire the mingling of pathos and declamation we find in *Atala* verges perilously on the comic.

Rather than a novel, *Atala* may be considered a tone poem in a minor key, and it is only by adapting ourselves to its mood that we can hope to appreciate its beauty. A random sampling of the work may seem melodramatic or false. But once we accept its conditions the difficulties fade, the natural man and the hermit's God are reconciled, highly refined feelings no longer seem strange in Indians, and we can even accept the compartmentlike structure of the work, the unnecessary coincidences, and the incredibility of numerous details.

And an exciting panorama then opens before us. Few writers match the skill of Chateaubriand in setting the stage, creating an atmosphere, and producing situations of dramatic intensity. Doubtless he was influenced in his descriptions by Rousseau, by Bernardin de Saint-Pierre's *Paul and Virginia,* and by Marmontel's *Incas,* and he copied such travelers as William Bartram, Jonathan Carver, and Charlevoix. But Rousseau's descriptions are still rhetorical and even those of Bernardin de Saint-Pierre pale before the vitality of Chateaubriand's evocations. Of equal talent are the pictorial passages where the author abandons himself to a mood of harmony with nature, and paints not with brilliant colors but ineffable half tones. His dramatic sequences, with their suspense and change of pace, inject movement into the plot.

Few of *Atala's* elements have escaped condemnation or ridicule. Seventy-five pages of creation have produced volumes of criticism. But the vitality of the work may be measured by the vigor of the criticism. The author's many defects are overshadowed by his talent. And such is the quality of his creation that even today, when much of the subject matter and style is dated, *Atala* may still be read with pleasure and sympathy.

René presents a very different problem, for here the matter is primarily moral. "Great writers have put their own story into their works," wrote Chateaubriand, and in certain respects *René* constitutes a miniature of the first three books of his *Memoirs.* The malady which afflicts René, then, was intimately felt by the author himself. He was not the first to experience it, for Goethe in the *Sorrows of Werther* and Senancour in *Musings on the Primitive Nature of Man* (1799) had dealt with analogous states of mind, and even Rousseau and Bernardin de Saint-Pierre had known emotions related to those of René. Soon afterwards were to come the intellectual *Obermann* of Senancour, the analytical *Adolphe* of Benjamin Constant, and *Childe Harold* of Byron. But René was not only the most intense and brilliant portrayal of the lassitude of living, it also had the advantage, like *Atala,* of appearing at the perfect moment. Like *Atala* it had been written mainly during the author's exile in England when poverty, loneliness and illness with the possibility of early death beset the young nobleman. The revolution had brought the world of Chateaubriand's childhood down in ruins. Along with others of his generation he was to feel a profound disorientation in a new type of society, whose values were unfamiliar and whose movements were unpredictable. In 1802, therefore, and in decades to come, *René* became for many young Frenchmen a kind of wish fulfillment, the most complete and faithful embodiment of a widespread psychological maladjustment.

To be sure, when observed from the individual point of view, the sadness of René is far less amenable to analysis. Neither its origin nor its precise nature can be clearly determined. The author, we have seen, apparently means to attribute a transcendental nature to it. Actually René's dissatisfaction is rooted in flagrant egoism. The experience of others seems irrelevant. His own instinctive reaction is perpetual retirement—to past civilizations, to the suburb, to the country, to America, or to suicide. As with his romantic brothers Obermann, Adolphe, Rolla, or Chatterton, his refusal to engage in any "practical" activity is an implicit revolt against society. Since he does nothing, he thus insures that he will never do anything "great or noble or just."

But there is an almost voluptuous compensation for this. René finds true satisfaction in his hours of endless introspection. Indeed, the "ordinary" misfortunes soon seem unworthy to him. Great sorrow becomes a method of individualizing oneself, of asserting one's existence as being apart from and superior to the rest of mankind. Suffering is less the law of life than the privilege of the exceptional individual. This is what distinguishes Chateaubriand from true pessimists.

Though the art of *René* necessarily differs from that of *Atala,* the same pictorial and dramatic talents are exploited to fix the image of the romantic. The stormy backgrounds, the sad but stimulating autumns, and the setting suns soon became familiar scenery. The figure of René brooding about destiny at the mouth of the crater, or striding along feverishly with the wind whistling through his hair, or stripping a willow branch and anxiously watching the leaves float downstream—images which were accepted at the time as lofty and which today seem so hollow—these tell us more about the romantic's feelings than any possible analysis.

The influence of Chateaubriand has been far-reaching. He pointed out to the nineteenth century new literary directions, and set up as its essential goal the elaboration of beauty. Vague, idealistic religiosity became an accepted literary theme, and Lamartine often seems to be fashioning into verse what Chateaubriand had said in poetic prose. The brilliantly colored "paintings" of Chateaubriand were impressed on the consciousness of descriptive artists including Victor Hugo (whose youthful ambition was to be "Chateaubriand or nothing"). Even historians were inspired: Augustin Thierry discovered his vocation in *The Martyrs*, and Michelet's manner is related to that of Chateaubriand. The feeling for nature received a strong new impetus from such writings as *Atala*.

The effect of *René* was even more profound and durable. The self-centered, mysterious, passionate, and uncompromising romantic hero of the early nineteenth century stems from René. Hernani, Antony, and Childe-Harold are only some of his relatives. Madame de Staël, Lamartine, Sainte-Beuve, George Sand, and even Flaubert have written about the emotion they experienced in reading *René*. A multitude of readers among the young generation were impressed by René's proud and melancholy attitude and often imitated it. Father Souël had, of course, reprimanded René at the end of the work, but this was swept away in the enthusiasm for the "new vice." Chateaubriand himself decried in his *Memoirs* the fashion he had created. "If *René* did not exist," he tells us, "I would no longer write it; if I could destroy it, I would. A family of René poets and René prose writers has been swarming about. We can hear nothing now but pitiful and disconnected phrases; they talk of nothing but winds and storms, and mysterious words whispered to the clouds and to the night. There is not a scribbler just out of school who hasn't dreamed of being the unhappiest man on earth, not an upstart of sixteen who hasn't exhausted life and felt himself tormented by his genius, who, in the abyss of his thoughts, hasn't given himself up to his vague passion, struck his pale and disheveled brow, and astounded men with sorrow which neither he nor they could describe."

These are vigorous terms, worthy of the creator of Aubry and Souël. But they reached the public a half century after *René,* when the "damage" was already done. René must remain as the model of the romantic hero in France. When Chateaubriand combined *René* with *Atala* in a separate edition of 1805, he was in fact offering to the reading public, in the hundred-odd pages of these "burning twins," all the major elements of the nascent romantic movement. It is impossible to understand French literature from 1800 to 1850 without Chateaubriand. He breathed new life into the spirit of France, and created in *Atala* and *René* two of its permanent literary landmarks.

Atala

PROLOGUE

In days gone by, France possessed a vast empire
in North America, extending from Labrador to the Floridas* and from the shores of the Atlantic to the most remote
lakes of Upper Canada.

Four great rivers, originating in the same mountains,
divide these huge regions: the Saint Lawrence River, which
empties in the east into the gulf of the same name; the
River of the West, which bears its waters away to unknown
seas; the Bourbon River, which plunges northward into
Hudson Bay, and the Meschacebe, which flows south into
the Gulf of Mexico.

This last-named river, in its course of over a thousand
leagues, waters a delightful country, which the inhabitants
of the United States call New Eden, while the French have
bequeathed to it the gentle name of Louisiana. A thousand
other rivers, all tributaries of the Meschacebe—the Mis-
souri, the Illinois, the Akanza, the Ohio, the Wabash, the
Tenase—enrich it with their silt and fertilize it with their
waters. When all these rivers are swollen with the winter
floods, when storms have leveled entire sections of the forests, the uprooted trees collect in the streams. Soon the mud
cements them, vines bind them together, and finally plants
take root everywhere and solidify the remains. Swept along
by the foam-crested waves, these masses move down to the
Meschacebe. The river takes hold of them and carries them
down to the Mexican gulf, where it leaves them on the
sandy banks, thus multiplying its mouths. At times it lifts
its voice as it passes the hills, and pours its flood waters
around the forest colonnades and the pyramids of Indian
tombs; it is the Nile of the wilderness. But grace is always
joined with splendor in scenes of nature. While the middle

* Author's and translator's notes will be found following the text.

current is pushing dead trunks of pines and oak trees down to the sea, floating islands of pistia and water lilies, their yellow blossoms rising like little banners, drift upstream along the banks in the two side currents. Green serpents, blue herons, pink flamingoes, and young crocodiles take passage on these floral vessels, and the entire colony, unfurling in the wind its golden sails, drifts, sunken in sleep, to a landing in some hidden cove of the river.

The two banks of the Meschacebe present the most extraordinary picture. On the western shore, savannahs spread out as far as the eye can see, and their verdant swells, receding in the distance, seem to rise into the blue of the sky where they fade from view. In these endless prairies herds of three or four thousand wild buffaloes wander about aimlessly. Occasionally a bison heavy with years breasts the waves and finds repose among the high grasses of some island in the Meschacebe. By his brow crowned with twin crescents, by his ancient, muddy beard, he might be taken for the god of the river, casting a satisfied eye over the grandeur of his waters and the wild abundance of his shores.

Such is the scene on the western bank; but it changes on the opposite side, and the two shores form an admirable contrast. Overhanging the streams, grouped together on rocks and mountains and scattered in the valleys, trees of every shape, of every hue and every odor, grow side by side and tangle together as they tower up to heights which weary the eye. Wild vines, bignonias and colocynths, twine around the foot of these trees, scale the boughs and crawl out to the tips of the branches, swinging from the maple to the tulip tree and from the tulip tree to the hollyhock, forming a thousand bowers, a thousand vaults and a thousand porticoes. Many times, as they stray from tree to tree, these vines throw floral arches across the arms of rivers. From the heart of these clumps the magnolia raises its motionless cone; capped with great white blossoms, it commands the entire forest, with no other rival than the palm tree, which gently waves its verdant fans beside it.

A host of animals placed by the Creator's hand in these retreats radiate gladness and life. Down avenues of trees, bears may be seen drunk with grapes, and reeling on the branches of the elm trees; caribou bathe in the lake; black squirrels frolic in the thick foliage; mocking birds and Virginia doves no larger than sparrows fly down to grass patches red with strawberries; green parrots with yellow heads, crimson-tinged woodpeckers and fire-bright cardinals spiral up to the tops of the cypresses; hummingbirds sparkle on the jasmine of the Floridas, and bird-catching serpents hiss as they swing, like lianas, from the forest domes.

While in the savannahs beyond the river everything is permeated with silence and calm, here, on the contrary, everything stirs and murmurs. Beaks pecking against the trunks of oak trees, the rustle of animals moving about or grazing or grinding fruit stones between their teeth, the rippling of waves, feeble moanings, muffled bellowings and gentle cooings, all fill this wilderness with a primitive and tender harmony. But should any breeze happen to stir up these solitudes, rocking these floating forms, confusing these masses of white and blue and green and pink, mingling all the colors and combining all the murmurs, then there emerge from the depths of the forest such sounds, and the eyes behold such sights, that it would be futile for me to attempt their description to those who have never themselves passed through these primeval fields of nature.

After the discovery of the Meschacebe by Père Marquette and the unfortunate La Salle, the first Frenchmen who settled at Biloxi and New Orleans formed an alliance with the Natchez, an Indian nation with formidable power in those territories. Disputes and jealousies later plunged the hospitable land into bloody strife. Among those Indians there was an old man named Chactas, whose age, wisdom, and vast knowledge of life had made him the patriarch of the wilderness, beloved of all. Like all men, he had acquired his great virtue at the price of suffering. Not only were the forests of the New World filled with his sorrows, but he had borne them even to the shores of France. After being held prisoner in the galleys of Marseilles through a cruel injustice, he was set free and later presented to Louis XIV. He had spoken with the great men of the age and had been present at the celebrations of Versailles, the tragedies of Racine, and the funeral orations of Bossuet. In short, this savage had beheld society at the pinnacle of its splendor.

And now, back in the bosom of his homeland, Chactas had enjoyed repose for several years. Nonetheless, heaven exacted a heavy price for this favor, for the old man had lost his sight. A young girl accompanied him over the slopes along the Meschacebe, just as Antigone once guided the steps of Oedipus over Mount Cytheron, and as Malvina led Ossian over the rocks of Morven.

In spite of the many injustices which Chactas had suffered at the hands of the French, he loved them. He still remembered Fénelon, who had once been his host, and he wished he could render some service to the countrymen of such a righteous man. An opportunity arose in 1725 when a Frenchman named René, impelled by passion and sorrow, arrived in Louisiana. He ascended the Meschacebe as far as the land of the Natchez, and asked to be admitted as one of their warriors. Chactas questioned him closely, and, finding him unshakeable in his resolution, adopted him as his son and gave him as a wife an Indian girl named Celuta. Soon after the marriage, the Indians made ready for the beaver hunt.

Although blind, Chactas was designated by the council of sachems as leader of the expedition, because of the high respect he commanded among the Indian tribes. Fasting and prayers began; the medicine men interpreted dreams; the manitous were consulted, and sacrifices of tobacco were offered; elk tongues were burned and carefully examined to see if they crackled in the flames, for thus could the will of the spirits be divined; and finally, after partaking of the sacred dog, the party set forth. René was among them. With the help of countercurrents, the pirogues ascended the

Meschacebe and entered the channel of the Ohio. It was autumn. The magnificent wilds of Kentucky spread out before the eyes of the astonished young Frenchman. One moonlit night, while the Natchez were all asleep in their pirogues and the Indian fleet was skimming along in a light breeze under its sails of animal skins, René, alone with Chactas, asked to hear the story of his adventures. The old man consented, and, sitting with him there at the stern of the pirogue, began his tale in the following words.

THE TALE

The Hunters

It is a strange fate, my dear son, which has brought us together. I see in you the civilized man who has become a savage; you see in me the savage whom the Great Spirit has (I know not for what purpose) chosen to civilize. Having entered life's path from opposite ends, you have now come to rest in my place while I have gone to sit in yours. And so we must have had a totally different view of things. Which of us has gained or lost more by this change of position? That is something which only the spirits know, for the least wise among them possesses greater wisdom than all men together.

At the next moon of flowers it will be seven times ten snows and three snows more since my mother bore me on the banks of the Meschacebe. The Spaniards had recently settled in the Bay of Pensacola, but no white man had yet come to dwell in Louisiana. I had seen the leaves falling barely seventeen times when I marched with my father, the warrior Outalissi, against the powerful Muskogees of the Floridas. We united with our allies, the Spaniards, and gave battle on one of the branches of the Mobile. Areskoui and the manitous were not propitious. The enemy was victorious, and my father lost his life, while I was twice wounded defending him. Oh! Why could I not then have descended to the land of souls! I would have avoided all the sorrows awaiting me on earth. The spirits willed it otherwise; I was swept along with the refugees to Saint Augustine.

In that city, newly built by the Spaniards, I ran the risk of being taken off to work in the mines of Mexico, when an old Castilian, named Lopez, who was touched by my youth and simplicity, offered me a haven and introduced me to his sister with whom he lived, as he was not married.

Both of them grew to have the most tender feelings for me. They brought me up with great care and gave me all kinds of teachers. But, after spending thirty moons in Saint Augustine, I was overcome by a strong distaste for the life of the city. Visibly I was wasting away. At times I remained motionless for hours contemplating the summit of distant forests; at other times I would be found on the bank of a river sadly watching it flow by. I pictured to myself the woods through which these waters had passed, and my soul was wholly given up to solitude.

No longer able to resist my desire to return to the wilderness, I appeared one morning before Lopez, dressed in my Indian clothes, holding my bow and arrows in one hand and my European garments in the other. These last I returned to my generous protector and fell at his feet, with tears streaming down my cheeks. I called myself hateful names and accused myself of ingratitude. "But in spite of everything," I said, "O father! You can see for yourself, I shall die if I do not go back to my Indian life."

Struck with surprise Lopez sought to dissuade me. He pointed out the dangers I would face if I again risked falling into the hands of the Muskogees. But, at last, seeing that I was resolved to attempt anything, he burst into tears and pressed me in his arms. "Go, son of nature!" he cried. "Go back to man's freedom; I do not wish to rob you of it. If I were younger myself, I would accompany you into the wilderness—for I too have sweet memories of it!—and I would restore you to your mother's arms. When you are back in your forests, think occasionally of this old Spaniard who showed you hospitality, and always remember—for it will help you to love your fellowmen—that your first experience with the human heart was all in its favor." Lastly, Lopez prayed to the God of the Christians, whose faith I had refused to embrace, and we parted sobbing.

It was not long before I was punished for my ingratitude.

Inexperienced as I was, I soon lost my way in the woods and was captured by a band of Muskogees and Seminoles, just as Lopez had predicted. I was recognized as a Natchez by my dress and the feathers adorning my head. They bound me, but only lightly, because I was young. Simaghan, the chief of the party, wished to know my name. I replied, "I am called Chactas, son of Outalissi, son of Miscou, who captured more than a hundred scalps from Muskogee heroes." Simaghan said to me, "Chactas, son of Outalissi, son of Miscou, rejoice; you shall be burned in the big village." "That is well," I answered, and I intoned my song of death.

Prisoner though I was, I could not help admiring my enemies during those first few days. The Muskogee, and particularly his ally the Seminole, breathes joy, affection, and contentment. His gait is nimble, his manner open and serene. He talks a great deal and fluently. His language is harmonious and smooth. Not even old age can rob the sachems of this joyous simplicity. Like the aged birds in our woods, they continue to blend their ancient songs with the fresh melodies of their young offspring.

The women accompanying the party treated me with tender pity and affectionate curiosity because of my youth. They questioned me about my mother and about the earliest days of my life. They wanted to know if my cradle of moss had hung from the flowering branches of the maple tree, and if breezes had rocked me beside nests of little birds. Then there were a thousand questions about the feelings in my heart. They asked me if I had seen a white doe in my dreams and if the trees in the secret valley had counseled me to love. I spoke naïvely to these mothers and daughters and wives of men. I said to them, "You are the graces of the day, and like the dew you are beloved of the night. Man issues from your womb only to cling to your breast and to your lips. You know magic words to lull all sorrows to sleep. This is what I was told by the one who gave me life and who will never again see me! She told me, too, that maidens are mysterious flowers found in solitary places."

These words of praise brought much pleasure to the women. They heaped all sorts of presents on me. They brought me nut cream and maple sugar, corn pudding, bear hams and beaver skins, shells to deck myself out and moss for my bed. They sang and they laughed with me, and then they shed tears as they remembered that I was soon to be burned.

One night, when the Muskogees had pitched camp at the edge of a forest, I was sitting near the war fire with the hunter assigned to guard me. Suddenly I heard the rustle of a garment in the grass, and a half-veiled woman came and sat down beside me. Tears were sparkling beneath her eyelids, and by the light of the fire I could see a little golden crucifix shining on her breast. She had beautiful, regular features, and in her face there was a certain virtuous, passionate quality impossible to resist. But she also possessed more tender charms, for extreme sensitivity and deep melancholy radiated from her eyes, and her smile was heavenly.

I thought she was the "Maiden of Last Love," sent to the prisoner of war to charm his grave. This filled me with uneasiness, though I had no fear of the stake, and I stammered out: "Maiden, you are worthy of a first love, you were not meant for the last. The feelings of a heart about to cease beating would hardly respond to the feelings of your own. How can we mingle life with death? You would make me too sad for the loss of my days. Let someone else be happier than I, and may the vine and the oak be joined in long embraces!"

Then the girl said: "I am not the 'Maiden of Last Love.' Are you a Christian?" I replied that I had not betrayed the spirits of my cabin. At these words the Indian girl started suddenly. She said to me: "I pity you for being no more than a wicked heathen. My mother made me a Christian; I am called Atala, daughter of Simaghan of the Golden Bracelets, who is chief of the warriors of this band. We are making our way to Apalachucla, where you will be burned." Pronouncing these words, Atala rose and went away.

Here Chactas was obliged to interrupt his tale. Memories were crowding into his mind, and from his sightless eyes tears streamed down his withered cheeks. It was as if two springs hidden deep in the blackness of the earth had revealed themselves by the waters filtering through the rocks.

Oh, my son, he continued at last, you see that Chactas is very unwise indeed, in spite of his wide reputation for wisdom! Alas, my dear child, even when men can no longer see they can still weep! Several days went by. The sachem's daughter came back each evening to speak to me. Sleep had fled from my eyes, and Atala was as dear to my heart as the memory of my parents' couch.

On the seventeenth day of the march, about the time when the dayfly appears from the waters, we came out onto the great Alachua savannah. It is encircled by hills retreating behind one another and bearing with them up to the clouds forest ranges of copalms, lemon trees, magnolias, and live oaks. The chief shouted the cry of arrival, and the band camped at the foot of the hills. I was relegated to a spot a certain distance away at the edge of one of the "natural wells" so famous in the Floridas. I was attached to the foot of a tree, and a warrior kept impatient watch over me. Hardly had I spent a few moments in this place, when Atala appeared under the liquidambars of the spring. "Hunter," she said to the Muskogee hero, "if you wish to pursue the roebuck, I will guard the prisoner." On hearing these words from the chief's daughter, the warrior leaped up with joy and sped down from the hilltop, bounding out into the plain with great strides.

What a strange contradiction is the heart of man! I had so keenly desired to reveal things of mystery to the one I already loved like the sun, and now I was speechless and troubled, and I think I would have preferred being thrown to the crocodiles in the stream to being alone with Atala. The daughter of the wilderness was as disturbed as her pris-

oner. We remained in deep silence; the Spirits of love had
stolen the words from our lips. At length Atala made an
effort, and spoke. "Warrior," she said, "you are bound
loosely; you can easily escape." At these words, boldness returned to my tongue, and I replied, "Loosely bound, O
woman!" But I could not finish. Atala hesitated a few moments, and then said, "Escape." And she untied me from the
trunk of the tree. I seized the rope and forced it back into
her hand, making her close her lovely fingers around my
bond. "Take it back! Take it back!" I cried. "You are mad,"
said Atala in a tremulous voice. "Poor man! Don't you know
you will be burned? What can you be thinking of? Are you
aware that I am the daughter of a formidable sachem?" With
tears in my eyes I replied: "There was a time when I too was
borne in a beaver skin on a mother's shoulders. My father
too had a fine cabin, and his deer drank the waters of a thousand streams. But now I wander about homeless. When I
am no more, there will be no friend to place a bit of grass on
my body to shield it from the flies. The body of an unhappy
stranger is of interest to no one."

These words touched Atala, and her tears dropped into
the spring. "Ah," I pressed on, "if your heart could speak
as does mine! Is the wilderness not free? Have the forests
no retreats to hide us away? Do children of the cabin need
so many things to make them happy! O maiden, more beautiful than the bridegroom's first dream! O my beloved!
Would you dare to follow my footsteps?" Those were my
words. Atala replied in a tender voice, "My young friend,
you have learned the language of the white man; it is easy
to mislead an Indian girl." "What?" I exclaimed, "you call
me your young friend! Ah! If a poor slave could . . ." "Well,"
she said, bending toward me, "if a poor slave . . ." I went on
ardently, "Let a kiss give him proof of your faith!" Atala
yielded to my wish. As a fawn seems to cling to the flowers
of the pink lianas, grasping them with its fine tongue on the
steep mountain bank, so I remained suspended on the lips
of my beloved.

Alas! My dear son, sorrow is closely allied to pleasure! Who could have believed that the moment when Atala offered me that first token of her love would be the very one when my hopes would be shattered? Whitened hair of old Chactas, what was your astonishment when the sachem's daughter pronounced these words: "Handsome prisoner, I have rashly given in to your desire. But where will this passion lead us? My religion separates me from you forever . . . O my mother! What have you done?" Atala suddenly grew silent and held back I knew not what fatal secret about to fall from her lips. Her words plunged me into despair. "Well, then!" I cried, "I will be as cruel as you; I will not run away. You shall see me framed in fire, you shall hear the groaning of my flesh, and you will be filled with joy." Atala seized my hands in both of hers. "Poor young heathen," she exclaimed, "how I grieve for you! Would you have me weep my heart away? What a pity I cannot flee with you! Unhappy was the womb of your mother, O Atala! Why do you not hurl yourself to the crocodile in the stream?"

At that very moment, as sunset drew near, the crocodiles began sending forth their roars. Atala said to me: "Let us leave this place." I drew the daughter of Simaghan along with me to the foot of the hills, which formed verdant gulfs as their promontories jutted out into the savannah. All the wilderness was calm and glorious. The stork was calling from its nest. The woods echoed with the monotonous song of the quail, the whistling of the parakeets, the bellowing of the bison, and the whinnying of Seminole mares.

We walked in almost total silence. I stayed beside Atala, while she held the end of the rope, which I had made her take back. Sometimes tears came to our eyes, and sometimes we tried to smile. A glance lifted heavenward or fixed on the earth, an ear alert to the song of the bird, a gesture toward the setting sun, a hand tenderly pressed, a breast heaving and tranquil by turns, the names of Chactas and Atala softly repeated at intervals . . . O first walk of love, your memory must surely be powerful, since you still stir the heart of old Chactas after so many years of misfortune!

What enigmas men are when they are buffeted by passions! I had just abandoned the kindly Lopez, I had exposed myself to every danger for the sake of my freedom, and now, in an instant, a woman's glance had changed my desires, my intentions, my thoughts! Forgetting my country, my mother, my cabin, and the horrible death awaiting me, I had become indifferent to all that was not Atala. I was powerless to rise to a man's mature reason, for I had suddenly sunk into a kind of childishness, and, far from being able to save myself from the trials in store for me, I virtually needed someone to take care of my sleeping and feeding needs.

And so, after we had wandered about in the savannah, it was in vain that Atala threw herself at my knees and implored me once more to leave her. I declared that I would return to the camp alone if she refused to tie me up again at the foot of my tree. She was obliged to yield, hoping to persuade me another time.

On the morrow of this day which decided the fate of my life, we halted in a valley not far from Cuscowilla, the capital of the Seminoles. These Indians together with the Muskogees form the confederacy of the Creeks. The daughter of the land of palms came for me in the middle of the night and led me into a great pine forest, where she exhorted me once again to escape. Without a word, I took her hand in my own, and forced the poor harried doe to wander about with me in the forest.

It was a beauteous night. The Spirit of the Atmosphere was shaking out his blue tresses, pregnant with the scent of the pines, and we could breathe the tenuous odor of amber floating up from the crocodiles asleep beneath the tamarinds by the river. The moon shone down from the cloudless blue, and its pearl-gray light drifted over the hazy summit of the forest. No sound could be heard, save some vague far-away harmony permeating the depths of the woods. It was as though the soul of solitude were sighing through the entire expanse of the wilderness.

Among the trees we perceived a young man holding a

torch in his hand, who seemed like the Spirit of Spring hastening through the forests to rouse nature back to life. It was a suitor on his way to learn his fate in the cabin of his beloved.

If the maiden blows out the torch, she accepts her lover's wooing; but if she veils herself and will not blow it out, then a husband is rejected.

Gliding by in the shadows, the warrior was softly singing:

"I will hasten before the steps of day to the mountain top to seek out my lonely dove among the oaks of the forest.

"I have hung about her throat a necklace of shells; there are three red beads for my love, three purple ones for my fears, three blue ones for my hopes.

"Mila has the eyes of an ermine and the flowing hair of a field of rice. Her mouth is a pink shell set with pearls. Her two breasts are as two spotless kids, born the same day of a single mother.

"May Mila put out this torch! May her mouth cast over it a voluptuous shadow! I will make fertile her womb. The hope of the nation shall cling to her plenteous breast, and I will smoke my calumet of peace by the cradle of my son.

"Ah! Let me hasten before the steps of day to the mountain top to seek out my lonely dove among the oaks of the forest!"

So sang the young man, and his accents struck anxiety into the depths of my soul and changed Atala's countenance. We felt our clasped hands suddenly quiver. But our attention was drawn away from this scene to another one no less portentous.

We passed a child's grave, which served as the boundary between two nations. It had been placed alongside the road, according to custom, so that young women, going down to the spring, could draw into their bosom the soul of the innocent creature and thus restore it to the nation. There at that very moment were young wives longing for the sweetness of motherhood and attempting with open lips to enfold the soul of the little child, which they fancied they saw wandering amid the flowers. Then the true mother came and laid a sheaf of corn and some white lilies on the grave. She moistened the ground with her milk, sat down on the wet grass and spoke tenderly to her child:

"Why do I weep for you in your earthen cradle, O my newborn? When the little bird grows up, he must go in search of his food, and he finds in the wilderness many a bitter seed. You at least have never known tears; your heart has never been exposed to the withering breath of men. The bud which dries up in its sheath departs with all its perfume, as did you, O my son, with all your innocence. Happy are they who die in the cradle, for they have known only the smiles and kisses of a mother!"

Already subdued by our own feelings, we were now overwhelmed by these images of love and motherhood, which seemed to pursue us in this enchanted solitude. I carried Atala in my arms deep into the forest, where I told her things which today my lips would seek in vain. My dear son, the south wind loses its warmth as it passes over the icy mountains. The memory of love in an old man's heart is as the fire of day reflected in the moon's calm sphere when the sun has gone down and silence hovers over the huts of the Indians.

Who could save Atala now? What could prevent her from yielding to nature? Doubtless nothing but a miracle—and that miracle happened! Simaghan's daughter had recourse to the God of the Christians. Throwing herself upon the ground, she breathed a fervent prayer to her mother and to the Queen of Virgins. From that moment on, O René, I have marveled at that religion which, in the forests, in the very midst of all the privations of life, can lavish untold blessings on the unfortunate. It is a religion which sets its might against the torrent of passions and alone suffices to subdue them, though they be stirred by every circumstance—the seclusion of the woods, the absence of men, and the complicity of the shadows. Ah! How divine did that simple savage girl seem to me, the innocent Atala, kneeling there before an old fallen pine as though at the foot of an altar, offering prayers up to her God for an idolatrous lover! Her eyes, raised toward the star of night, and her cheeks, glistening with tears of love and divine faith, radiated immortal beauty. Several times I thought she was about to take flight toward the heavens; and again it seemed as though there were descending upon the moon's rays and rustling among the branches of the trees those spirits whom the Christian God sends to rock-dwelling hermits when He is about to summon them back to Himself. I was deeply grieved, for I feared that Atala had but little time left to remain on earth.

However, she shed so many tears and revealed her sorrow so plainly, that I might have consented to depart, when the cry of death rang out in the forest, and four armed men flung themselves upon me. We had been discovered, and the war chief had given orders to pursue us.

Atala resembled a queen in the pride of her bearing, disdaining to speak to these warriors. She cast a haughty glance at them, and went off to Simaghan.

She was unable to obtain any concession. My guards were doubled, my bonds multiplied, and my beloved separated from me. Thus five nights went by, and we came in sight of Apalachucla, situated on the banks of the Chattahoochee River. Immediately I was crowned with flowers, my face was painted with blue and vermilion, beads were fastened to my nose and ears, and a chichicoué was placed in my hand.

Thus decked out for the sacrifice I entered Apalachucla, accompanied by the repeated shouts of the throng. My fate was sealed—when suddenly the sound of a conch horn was heard, and the Mico, or chief of the nation, gave the order to assemble.

My son, you are acquainted with the torments to which savages subject their prisoners of war. Christian missionaries, at the risk of their lives and with tireless charity, had persuaded several nations to substitute a rather mild form of slavery for the horrors of the stake. The Muskogees had

not yet adopted this custom, but a great number had declared themselves in favor of it. It was to decide on this important matter that the Mico was now summoning the
sachems. I was led out to the place of deliberation.

Not far from Apalachucla, on an isolated knoll, rose the
council pavilion. Three circles of columns formed the ele-
gant architecture of this rotunda. The columns were made
of polished and carved cypress, increasing in height and
thickness and diminishing in number as they approached
the center, which was marked by a single pillar. From the
top of this pillar, strips of bark projected over the tops of
the other columns, covering the pavilion in the form of an
open fan.

The council assembled. Fifty elders in beaver robes ar-
ranged themselves in tiers facing the entrance of the pavilion. In the middle sat the high chieftain, holding in his
hand the calumet of peace, half colored for war. At the right
of the elders fifty women dressed in robes of swan feathers
took their places. The war chiefs, tomahawk in hand and
headdress in place, their arms and chests stained with blood,
occupied the left section.

At the foot of the central column burned the council fire.
The chief medicine man, dressed in long garments with a
stuffed owl on his head, and surrounded by the eight guard-
ians of the temple, poured balsam of the copalm over the
flames and offered up a sacrifice to the sun. These triple
rows of elders, matrons, and warriors, these priests, these
clouds of incense, this sacrifice—everything here contributed to the council's august setting.

I stood bound in the midst of the assembly. When the
sacrifice had been consummated, the Mico raised his voice
and in simple terms presented the question which had
brought the council together. Then he threw a blue necklace into the gathering in testimony of what he had just said.

Thereupon a sachem of the Eagle tribe rose and spoke:

"Father Mico, sachems, matrons, warriors of the four
tribes of the Eagle, the Beaver, the Serpent and the Tor-

toise, let us not alter the customs of our ancestors; let us burn the prisoner, instead, and not soften our courage. This custom which you are asked to accept is a white man's custom; it cannot fail to be harmful. Offer a red necklace containing my words. I have spoken."

And he threw a red necklace into the assembly.

A matron then rose and said:

"Father Eagle, you have the mind of a fox and the measured prudence of a tortoise. I would polish the chain of friendship with you, and together we will plant the tree of peace. But let us change the customs of our ancestors when they are destructive. Let us have slaves to cultivate our fields, and let us hear no more the shrieks of prisoners which disturb the breasts of our mothers. I have spoken."

As the waves of the sea are shattered in a storm, as the withered leaves are whirled away by the autumn wind, as the reeds of the Meschacebe bend and straighten up in a sudden overflow, as a great herd of deer bell in the depths of the woods, so did that council stir and murmur. Sachems, warriors, and matrons spoke out in turn or else all together. Interests clashed, opinions were divided, and the council was on the verge of breaking up, but in the end the ancient custom prevailed and I was condemned to the stake.

One circumstance postponed my ordeal. The Ceremony for the Dead or Rites for Departed Souls was approaching, and it is customary not to put a captive to death during the days dedicated to this ceremony. I was entrusted to a strict guard, and the sachems apparently sent Simaghan's daughter away, for I saw her no more.

Meanwhile the nations for more than three hundred leagues around were streaming in to celebrate the Rites for Departed Souls. A long cabin had been built in a remote spot. On the designated day, each family unearthed the remains of its forefathers from their individual graves, and their skeletons were hung, in order of rank and family, along the walls of the Ancestral Community Chamber. A storm had arisen, and the winds, forests, and waterfalls were roaring outside, as the elders of the different nations concluded treaties of peace and alliance with each other over the bones of their forebears.

Then came the celebration with funeral contests, races, ball games, and knuckle-bones. Two girls vied with each other to snatch away a willow rod. The buds of their breasts approached and touched; their hands spun around on the rod, raising it above their heads. Their fine bare feet engaged each other, their mouths met, their sweet breaths merged, and they leaned over and mingled their hair. Then they glanced at their mothers and blushed, and they were applauded. The medicine man invoked Michabou, the spirit of the waters. He related the wars of the Great Hare against Matchimanitou, the god of evil. He told of the first man and Atahensic the first woman, cast out of heaven for having lost their innocence, of the earth reddened with blood spilled by a brother, of Jouskeka the impious, murdering the righteous Tahouistsaron, of the flood coming down at the bidding of the Great Spirit, of Massou saved alone in his bark canoe, and of the raven sent out to discover the land. He told also of the beautiful Endaë, recalled from the land of souls by the sweet songs of her husband.

After these games and hymns, they prepared to give their ancestors an everlasting burial.

On the banks of the Chattahoochee River there was a wild fig tree hallowed by the faith of those peoples. The young girls used to wash their bark dresses at this spot, exposing them to the breath of the wilderness on the branches of the venerable tree. It was there that an enormous grave had been hollowed out. The procession set forth from the funeral chamber, chanting the hymn of death, with each family bearing its sacred remains. They arrived at the grave, and the relics were lowered in, spread out in layers, and separated by bear and beaver skins. A mound rose over the tomb, and the Tree of Tears and Sleep was planted upon it.

Men must be pitied, my dear son! Those very Indians whose customs are so moving, those very women who had

treated me with such tender concern, now were calling
loudly for my execution, and entire nations delayed their
departure in order to have the pleasure of seeing a young
man suffer frightful torments.

In a valley to the north, at some distance from the great
village, stood a clump of cypress and pine trees, called the
"Wood of Blood." The approach to it led through the ruins
of one of those monuments whose origin is unknown and
whose builders are now forgotten. In the center of these
woods was a clearing where prisoners of war were sacrificed.
I was led there in triumph. All was made ready for my death.
The stake of Areskoui was driven into the ground, pine
trees, elms, and cypresses fell under the axe, the funeral pile
was raised, and the spectators built amphitheaters with
branches and tree trunks. Each person devised a different
torture: one proposed tearing the skin off my skull, another
burning my eyes out with red hot hatchets. I began my song
of death.

"I fear no suffering, O Muskogees, I am brave! I defy you
and despise you more than women. My father Outalissi, son
of Miscou, drank from the skulls of your most famous warriors. You will not tear a single groan from my breast."

Provoked by my song, a warrior pierced my arm with an
arrow; I said, "Brother, I thank you."

But in spite of the executioners' activity, the preparations
for the torture could not be completed before sunset. The
medicine man was consulted, and he would not allow the
spirits of the shadows to be disturbed; thus, my death was
again postponed to the following day. But, in their impa-
tience to enjoy the spectacle and in their desire to be ready
immediately at daybreak, the Indians did not leave the
Wood of Blood; they lit great fires and began their festivi-
ties and dancing.

Meanwhile I had been stretched out on my back. Ropes
were passed around my neck, feet, and arms and then tied
to stakes driven in the ground. Several warriors lay down on
these ropes, and I could not budge without alerting them.

The night moved on. Gradually the songs and dances died away. The fires now cast only feeble ruddy glimmers, before which shadows of a few savages could still be seen flitting by. The whole camp grew drowsy. As the noise of man diminished, the sound of the wilderness grew stronger, and the tumult of voices was followed by the sighing of the wind in the forest.

It was the hour when a young Indian woman, who has just become a mother, starts from her sleep in the dead of night, for she thinks she has heard the cry of her first-born calling for his sweet nourishment. With my eyes fixed on the sky, where the crescent of the night was wandering among the clouds, I reflected on my fate. Atala seemed to me a monster of ingratitude, abandoning me thus at the supreme moment, after I had sacrificed myself to the flames rather than leave her side! And yet I felt I still loved her and would joyfully die for her.

In extreme pleasure there is a spur which alerts us and warns us to take advantage of the fleeting moment. But in great sorrow some mysterious heaviness lulls us to sleep; eyes weary with tears seek naturally to close—and thus is the loving-kindness of Providence apparent even in our misfortunes. I yielded, in spite of myself, to the torpid slumber which sometimes envelops those who suffer. I dreamed that my fetters were being removed, and I seemed to feel the relief which is experienced when a helping hand loosens our irons after we have been tightly bound.

This feeling became so intense that I was obliged to raise my eyelids. By the light of a moonbeam filtering between two clouds, I made out a large white figure leaning over me, silently untying my bonds. I was about to cry out, when a hand which I instantly recognized closed my mouth. A single rope still remained, but it seemed impossible to cut it without touching a warrior who was covering its whole length with his body. Atala placed her hand on it. The warrior half awakened and sat up. Atala remained motionless, watching him. The Indian thought he was looking at the

Spirit of the Ruins and lay down again, closing his eyes and invoking his Manitou. The bond was broken. I stood up and followed my deliverer, while she held out to me the end of a bow, keeping the other end herself. But what dangers still beset us! Sometimes we almost stumbled over sleeping savages; then a guard challenged us, and Atala replied disguising her voice. Children cried out and watch dogs barked. No sooner had we left the fatal circle than the forest shook with fearful howling. The camp awoke, a thousand fires went up, and everywhere savages were running with torches. We quickened our steps.

When dawn rose over the Appalachians, we were already far away. What was my joy to find myself once again alone with Atala, Atala my deliverer, who was giving herself to me forever! Words failed my lips; I fell to my knees, and said to the daughter of Simaghan: "Men are little indeed, but when the spirits come to them, then they are nothing at all. You are a spirit, you have come to me, and I am speechless before you." Atala smilingly held out her hand. "I must indeed follow you," she said, "since you refuse to flee without me. During the night I beguiled the medicine man with presents, I made your executioners drunk with fire water, and I had to risk my life for you, since you had given up your own for me. Yes, young heathen," she added in a tone which frightened me, "the sacrifice will be mutual."

Atala gave me the weapons she had taken care to bring along, and then she dressed my wound. As she was wiping it with a papaya leaf, her tears again moistened it. "You are spreading balm over my injury," I told her. "I am afraid it is poison instead," she replied. Tearing away one of the coverings of her breast, she made a first dressing, and tied it with a lock of her hair.

a bit overplayed i would say!

Drunkenness, which lasts a long time in savages and is a kind of sickness for them, must have prevented my captors from pursuing us during those first few days. If they looked for us afterward, it was probably toward the west, as they must have been convinced we had tried to head toward the

Meschacebe. But we had set our course in the direction of the fixed star, guiding ourselves by the moss on the tree trunks.

It was not long before we became aware of how little we had gained by my escape. The wilderness now spread its endless solitude before us. Inexperienced as we were in the life of the forest, turned aside from our proper path and walking at random, what would now become of us? Often, as I looked at Atala, I recalled the ancient story, which Lopez had given me to read, about Hagar in the wilderness of Beersheba a long, long time ago, when men lived to thrice the age of the oak tree.

As I was practically naked, Atala made me a cloak of the inner bark of the ash tree. She embroidered for me muskrat moccasins with porcupine hair. I, in turn, took care of her adornment. Sometimes I would place upon her head a coronet of blue mallows, which we found along the way in abandoned Indian cemeteries; I also made her necklaces of red azalea seeds, and then I would smile as I considered her marvelous beauty.

When we came to a river, we went across on a raft or else we swam. Atala would rest one of her hands on my shoulder, and we would glide through those lonely waves like two traveling swans.

In the intense heat of the day, we often sought shelter beneath the moss of the cedars. Almost all the trees in Florida, particularly the cedar and the live oak, are covered with a white moss hanging from the branches down to the ground. If at night, in the moonlight, you should notice a solitary holm rising out of the nakedness of the savannah, mantled in this drapery, you would think you were looking at a ghost trailing its long veils behind it. The scene is no less picturesque in the middle of the day, for a swarm of butterflies, bright insects, hummingbirds, green parakeets, and blue jays attaches itself to these mosses and produces the effect of a white wool tapestry embroidered by a European artisan with brilliantly colored birds and insects.

It was in the shade of these charming hostelries, prepared by the Great Spirit, that we sought repose. Whenever the wind swept out of the sky, rocking the great cedar, when the aerial castle built on its branches began swaying with the birds and other travelers asleep in its shelter, when a thousand sighs emerged from the corridors and vaults of the moving edifice, never could the wonders of the Old World approach this monument of the wilderness.

Each night we lit a great fire and built a traveling hut of bark raised on four posts. If I had killed a wild turkey, a wood pigeon, or a pheasant, we hung it over a burning oak, at the tip of a pole driven in the ground, and let the wind take care of turning the prey of my hunting. We ate mosses called "rock tripe," sweet birch bark, and May apples, which taste like peaches and raspberries. The black walnut, the maple, and the sumac supplied wine for our table. Sometimes I would go into the reeds and find a plant with a flower elongated in the form of a horn, containing a glass of the purest dew. Then we would bless Providence, which had placed this limpid spring on the slender stem of a flower in the midst of foul marshes, just as it places hope deep in hearts sore with sorrow and makes virtue spring from the bosom of life's miseries.

Alas! I soon discovered that I was mistaken about Atala's seeming calm. The further we went, the sadder she became. Often for no reason she would shudder and turn her head suddenly. I would surprise her fixing her eyes on me passionately and then turning them heavenward with profound melancholy. What especially frightened me was a certain secret, a thought hidden in the depths of her being, which I could just glimpse in her eyes. Repeatedly she attracted and repulsed me, raising and then crushing my hopes, so that every time I thought I had made some inroads into her heart, I found myself back where I had begun. How many times did she tell me:

"O my young lover! I love you as I love the shade of the woods at midday! You are handsome as the wilderness with all its flowers and breezes. If I bend toward you, I tremble; if my hand falls upon yours, I feel I am near death. The other day the wind blew your hair into my face as you lay resting on my bosom, and I thought I felt the gentle touch of invisible spirits. Yes, I have seen young goats on the mountain of Oconee, and I have heard the words of men sated with days, but the sweetness of the kids and the wisdom of the elders are less pleasing and less potent than your words. Ah, my poor Chactas, I shall never be your bride!"

The constant struggle between Atala's love and religion, her unrestrained tenderness and the purity of her ways, the pride of her character and her deep sensitivity, the loftiness of her soul in essential things and her delicacy in the little ones—everything made her an incomprehensible being. Atala's influence over a man could never be weak; she was as irresistible as she was passionate, and she had to be worshipped or hated.

After advancing rapidly for fifteen nights, we entered the range of the Alleghany Mountains and reached one of the branches of the Tenase, a river emptying into the Ohio. Guided by Atala's advice I built a canoe, sewing the bark together with fir roots and coating it with the gum of the plum tree. Then I embarked with Atala, and together we abandoned ourselves to the current of the river.

As we came round a promontory, the Indian village of Sticoe appeared on our left with its pyramidal tombs and ruined huts. On our right we passed the valley of Keowe, at the foot of which we could make out the cabins of Jore suspended on the brow of Jore Mountain. The river which was carrying us along flowed between high cliffs, beyond which we could see the setting sun. Those deep retreats were never disturbed by the presence of man. We saw but one Indian hunter, who stood motionless leaning on his bow at the tip of a crag looking like a statue erected in the mountain to the spirit of those wildernesses.

Atala and I joined our silence to the silence of this scene. Suddenly the daughter of exile pierced the winds with a

voice full of emotion and melancholy. She was singing of
the lost homeland.

"Happy are they who have never seen the smoke of the
stranger's celebrations and have sat only at the festivals of
their fathers!

"If the blue jay of the Meschacebe should say to the bunting of the Floridas: Why dost thou pine so sadly? Hast thou
not here cool waters and fine foliage and all manner of
nourishment as in thy forests? Yes, the exiled bunting would
reply, but my nest is in the jasmine; who will bring it to me?
And the sun of my savannah, dost thou have that?

"Happy are they who have never seen the smoke of the
stranger's celebrations and have sat only at the festivals of
their fathers!

"After wending his painful way many hours, the traveler
sits down quietly. He contemplates about him the roofs of
men; the traveler has no place to rest his head. The traveler
knocks at the cabin, he places his bow behind the door, he
asks for hospitality. The master makes a sign with his hand;
the traveler takes up his bow and returns to the wilderness!

"Happy are they who have never seen the smoke of the
stranger's celebrations and have sat only at the festivals of
their fathers!

"Wondrous stories told around the hearth, tender out-
pourings of the heart, long habits of loving so essential to
life, you have filled the days of those who have never left
their native land! Their graves are in their country with
the setting sun, the tears of their friends, and the spell of
religion.

"Happy are they who have never seen the smoke of the
stranger's celebrations and have sat only at the festivals of
their fathers!"

Thus sang Atala. Her plaint was unbroken save for the
imperceptible sound of our canoe on the waves. In two or
three places alone it was caught up by a faint echo, repeated
to a second even fainter, and then to a third fainter still.
It seemed as though two lovers, once luckless as we, had

been attracted by the touching melody and took pleasure in sighing forth its final tones in the mountain.

Meanwhile the solitude, the constant presence of the beloved, and even our sorrows intensified our love with every passing moment. Atala's strength was beginning to fail her, and the passions weakening her body seemed about to overcome her resistance. She prayed continually to her mother, whose angered shade she seemed anxious to appease. Sometimes she would ask me if I could not hear a plaintive voice or see flames shooting out of the earth. As for me, exhausted with fatigue but still burning with desire and reflecting that I was perhaps hopelessly lost in the midst of those forests, a hundred times I was on the verge of seizing my bride in my arms, and a hundred times I suggested that we build a hut on those shores and hide ourselves away forever. But still she resisted me. "Remember, my young friend," she said, "a warrior is bound to his country. What is a woman beside the duties you must fulfill? Take courage, son of Outalissi; do not complain of your fate. The heart of man is like the river sponge, which drinks the pure wave in times of calm, and swells with mire when the sky has troubled the waters. Does the sponge have the right to say: I thought there would never be storms and the sun would never be scorching?"

O René! If you dread the agitations of the heart, beware of solitude. Great passions are solitary, and when you take them out into the wilderness you are setting them into their very own sphere. Overwhelmed as we were with care and fear, in constant peril of falling into the hands of hostile Indians, of being swallowed up by the waters, bitten by serpents or devoured by beasts, finding our meager fare with great difficulty and not knowing where next to turn our steps, we thought it impossible for our sorrows to increase, and then they were brought to a climax by chance.

It was the twenty-seventh sun since we had left the cabins, the "moon of fire" had begun its course, and everything foreshadowed a thunderstorm. Towards the hour when In-

dian matrons hang their plow staff on the branches of the
juniper and the parakeets retire into the hollows of the
cypresses, the sky began to cloud over. The voices of the
solitude died away, the wilderness grew still and the forests
hung in universal calm. Soon the rumblings of distant thunder began reverberating in these age-old woods, issuing forth
in sublime resonances. Afraid of being drowned, we hastily
made for the river bank and took shelter in the forest.

We now found ourselves in marshy terrain. With difficulty we pressed ahead under an archway of greenbrier,
among vines and indigo plants, bean stalks and crawling
lianas, which entangled our feet like nets. The spongy earth
trembled all around us, and we were constantly in danger
of being sucked down in quagmires. Innumerable insects
and huge bats blinded us; everywhere rattlesnakes were hissing, and wolves, bears, little tigers, and wolverines, coming
to take refuge, filled these retreats with their roars.

Meanwhile it grew much darker, and the lowering clouds
moved in among the dense woods. Suddenly the heavens
burst open, and a fiery shaft of lightning flashed through
the sky. A fierce wind sprang out of the west, rolling up
cloud over cloud. The whole forest bent, the sky split apart
again and again, and through its rifts appeared new heavens
and blazing vistas. Frightful, magnificent spectacle! The
thunderbolt set fire to the woods, and the burning expanse
spread like a flaming mass of hair. Flashing, fuming columns
besieged the heavens, which vomited bolts of lightning into
the vast conflagration. Then the Great Spirit covered the
mountains with heavy shadows. From the midst of this vast
chaos rose a confused uproar formed by the crashing winds,
the moaning trees, the howling of fierce beasts, the crackling
of the conflagration, and the constant flashing of the lightning hissing as it plunged into the waters.

At that moment, the Great Spirit knows, there was nothing before my eyes nor in my thoughts save Atala. Beneath
the sagging trunk of a birch I succeeded in shielding her
from the torrential downpour. As I sat there under the

tree, holding my beloved on my knees and warming her naked feet in my hands, I was happier than the young bride feeling the first thrill of her offspring in her womb.

We were listening to the roar of the storm, when suddenly I felt a tear fall on my breast. "Tempest of the heart," I cried, "is this a drop of your rain?" Then I pressed my beloved to me tightly and said: "Atala, you are hiding something from me. Open your heart, O my beauty! It is so consoling to have a friend look into our soul! Tell me what secret sorrow you insist on concealing. Ah! I can see, you are pining for your country." Immediately she replied, "Son of men, how could I pine for my country when my father did not come from the land of the palms?" "What!" I answered in great surprise, "your father was not from the land of the palms! Who, then, was the man who summoned you to earth? Tell me." Then Atala spoke these words:

"Before my mother brought the warrior Simaghan her marriage offering of thirty mares, twenty buffaloes, a hundred measures of acorn oil, fifty beaver skins and many other riches, she had known a man of white flesh. My mother's mother cast water in her face and obliged her to marry the magnanimous Simaghan, who is so like a king and honored by nations like a spirit. But my mother said to her new husband: 'My womb has conceived, now kill me.' Then Simaghan answered: 'May the Great Spirit preserve me from anything so wicked! I shall not disfigure you, nor shall I cut off your nose or your ears, because you have been sincere and have not dishonored my couch. The fruit of your body shall be my fruit, and I shall not visit you until the bird of the rice fields has flown and the thirteenth moon has begun to shine.' When the time came, I emerged from my mother's womb, and as I grew, my Spanish and Indian pride grew with me. My mother made me a Christian, so that her God and the God of my father would also be my God. Then the sorrow of love sought her out, and she went down to the narrow skin-lined hollow from which no one ever returns."

Such was Atala's story. "And who was your father, poor orphan?" I said. "How is he known by men on earth and what name did he bear among the spirits?" "I have never washed my father's feet," said Atala. "I know only that he lived with his sister in Saint Augustine and has always been faithful to my mother. Philip was his name among the angels, and men called him Lopez."

At these words a cry escaped me which rang through the solitude, and my ecstatic outbursts mingled with the din of the storm. Clasping Atala to my heart I cried out between my sobs: "O my sister! O daughter of Lopez! Daughter of my benefactor!" Atala was alarmed and wished to know why I was so excited. But when she discovered that Lopez was the host who had so generously adopted me in Saint Augustine, and whom I had left in order to be free, she too was overcome with confusion and joy.

This fraternal affection which had come upon us, joining its love to our own love, proved too powerful for our hearts. Atala's struggle was now to be futile! It was in vain that I felt her lift her hand to her bosom in an extraordinary gesture. Already I had caught her in my arms, already I had thrilled to her breath and drunk deep of love's magic on her lips. With my eyes lifted heavenward, I held my bride in my arms by the light of the flashing thunderbolts and in the presence of the Eternal. Nuptial ceremony, worthy of our sorrows and the grandeur of our passion! Glorious forests, waving your vines and leafy domes as curtains and canopy for our couch, blazing pines forming the torches of our wedding, flooded river, roaring mountains, O dreadful, sublime Nature, were you no more than a device contrived to deceive us, and could you not for an instant conceal a man's joy in your mysterious horrors?

Atala could offer only feeble resistance, and the ecstatic moment had come, when suddenly an impetuous bolt of lightning, followed by a clap of thunder, furrowed the thickness of the shadows, filled the forest with fire and brimstone, and split a tree apart at our very feet. We fled away. Oh, the surprise! . . . There in the ensuing silence we heard the ringing of a bell! Astounded we both strained to hear this sound, so strange in the wilderness. A moment later a dog was barking in the distance; as he approached, his yelps grew louder, until finally he reached our feet, howling with joy. An aged recluse, bearing a small lantern, was following him through the gloom of the forest. "Heaven be blessed!" he cried out as soon as he had caught sight of us. "I have been seeking you for a long, long time! Our dog picked up your scent at the beginning of the storm, and he has brought me here. Bountiful God! How young they are, poor children! How they must have suffered! Come! I have brought with me a bear skin—it will be for the young woman; and here is a little wine in our calabash. God be praised in all His works! His mercy is great indeed, and His goodness is infinite!"

At once Atala was at the holy man's feet. "Guide of prayer," she said, "I am a Christian. Heaven has sent you to save me." "My daughter," said the hermit raising her to her feet, "we regularly ring the mission bell during the night and in storms to summon strangers, and like our brethren in Lebanon and the Alps, we have taught our dog to search out travelers gone astray."

I could scarcely understand the hermit. Such charity seemed so far superior to mortal man that I thought I was in a dream. By the light of the little lantern in the holy man's hand I could see that his beard and hair were wet through. His feet, hands, and face were all blood-stained from the brambles. "Old man," I finally exclaimed, "how strong of heart must you be, since you have no fear of being struck down by the lightning?" "Fear!" replied the father with a kind of intense fervor, "shall I fear when men are in peril and I can be useful to them! Surely I would be a most unworthy servant of Christ!" "But," I said, "are you aware that I am not a Christian?" "Young man," answered the hermit, "have I asked you your religion? Christ did not say, 'My blood shall wash this man and not that one.' He died for the Jew and the Gentile, and in all men he saw only brothers and sufferers. What I do for you here is little indeed, and elsewhere you would find greater succor. But no glory for this must fall upon priests. What are we but feeble recluses and imperfect instruments of a celestial work? Yes! And what soldier would be cowardly enough to draw back when his leader, cross in hand and brow crowned with thorns, marches before him to succor men?"

These words gripped my heart, and tears of admiration and tenderness fell from my eyes. "My dear children," said the missionary, "I govern a little flock of your Indian brethren in these forests. My grotto is nearby in the mountain. Come and warm yourselves in my dwelling. You will not find the comforts of life, but you will have a shelter, and even for that we must thank Divine Providence, for there are many men who have none."

The Tillers

There are righteous men whose conscience is so tranquil that one cannot approach them without sharing in the peace emanating from their hearts and from their words. As the hermit spoke, I felt the passions abating in my breast, and even the storm in the sky seemed to draw away at his voice. Soon the clouds were scattered enough to allow us to leave our shelter. We emerged from the forest and began climbing the slope of a high mountain. The dog went before us carrying the extinguished lantern at the end of a stick. I held Atala's hand, and together we followed the missionary. He turned around frequently to look at us, contemplating our sorrows and youth with pity. A book hung from his neck,

and he leaned on a white staff. His figure was tall, his face
pale and thin, and his expression simple and sincere. He did
not have the lifeless, indistinct features of a man born without passions; plainly his days had been hard, and the furrows
on his brow revealed the rich scars of passions healed by
virtue and by the love of God and man. As he spoke to us,
erect and motionless, his long beard, his eyes humbly
lowered, the affectionate tone of his voice, everything about
him possessed something strangely calm and sublime. Whoever has seen Father Aubry, as I have, wending his solitary
way in the wilderness with his staff and his breviary, has a
true idea of the Christian wayfarer on earth.

After picking our way dangerously along the mountain
paths for half an hour, we reached the missionary's grotto.
We went in through the wet ivy and gourds which the rain
had torn loose from the rocks. There was nothing inside
save a matting of papaya leaves, a calabash for drawing
water, a few wooden vessels, a spade, a tame snake, and, on
a block of stone serving as a table, a crucifix and the book
of the Christians.

The man of ancient days hastened to light a fire with dry
vines. Crushing some corn between two stones, he made a
cake which he set under the ashes to cook. When the fire
had given the cake a rich golden color, he served it to us
steaming hot with nut oil in a maple bowl.

Calm returned with the evening, and the servant of the
Great Spirit suggested that we go out and sit at the entrance
to the grotto. We followed him and looked out over a vast
scene. In the east the last remains of the storm were scattered in disorder; the fires set off by the lightning in the forest still glimmered in the distance; at the foot of the mountain, an entire pine wood had been leveled in the mud, and
the river was sweeping wet sod along pell-mell with tree
trunks, bodies of animals, and dead fish whose silvery bellies
could be seen floating on the surface of the waters.

It was in this setting that Atala told our story to the great
patriarch of the mountain. His heart appeared touched,

and tears fell upon his beard. "My child," he said to Atala, "you must offer your sufferings to God, for whose glory you have already done so much; He will restore your tranquillity. See how those forests are smoking, how those floods are drying, and those clouds vanishing. Do you think that He who can calm such a tempest cannot appease the torments of the human heart? If you have no better haven, my dear daughter, I can offer you a place among the flock I have been fortunate enough to call to Christ. I shall teach Chactas, and when he is worthy, I shall give him to you for a husband."

At these words I fell at the hermit's knees, shedding tears of joy—but Atala grew pale as death. The old man raised me benignly, and then I noticed that both his hands were mutilated. Atala instantly understood the sorrows he had been through. "Barbarians!" she cried out.

"My daughter," replied the father with a gentle smile, "what is this beside all that my divine Master bore? Heathen Indians have persecuted me, but they are poor, blind creatures whom God will one day enlighten. Indeed the more they have made me suffer the dearer I hold them. I had returned to my own land, but I could not remain there, though its renowned queen did me the honor of asking to see these meager signs of my apostolate. And what more glorious recompense could I receive for my work than permission from the head of our religion to celebrate the divine sacrifice with these mutilated hands? After such an honor, I could not but attempt to make myself worthy of it. I came back to the New World to use up the rest of my life in the service of my God. I have dwelt in these wilds almost thirty years, and it will be twenty-two years tomorrow that I adopted this rock as my home. When I arrived in this region, I found only wandering families with fierce customs and a pitiful way of life. I have given them an understanding of the word of peace, and their customs have gradually grown gentler. Now they live together at the foot of this mountain. While showing them the ways of salvation, I have also tried to teach them the basic arts of life, not taking them too far, and still preserving for these good people the simplicity which brings happiness. As for myself, I have been afraid of hampering them by my presence, and so I have withdrawn to this grotto, where they come to consult me. It is here, far from men, that I admire God in the grandeur of these solitudes, and prepare myself for death, which my old age announces."

On finishing these words, the recluse sank to his knees, and we followed his example. He began a prayer aloud, with Atala responding. Lightning still flashed silently across the heavens in the east, while over the western clouds three suns shone together. Some foxes scattered by the storm stretched their black snouts over the edge of the precipices, and shrubs could be heard rustling as they dried in the evening breeze and everywhere lifted up their fallen stalks.

We went back into the grotto, where the hermit spread a bed of cypress moss for Atala. Deep uneasiness was visible in the maiden's eyes and movements. She kept looking at Father Aubry as though she would communicate a secret to him, but something seemed to hold her back, perhaps my presence, perhaps a certain feeling of shame, or perhaps the very futility of the confession. I heard her rise in the dead of night, looking for the recluse, but as he had given her his sleeping place, he had gone off to contemplate the beauty of the heavens and pray to God on the mountain top. He told me the next day that this was a common habit of his even in the winter, as he loved to watch the forests waving their naked tree tops and the clouds fleeing across the skies while he listened to the winds and streams roaring in the solitude. And so my sister was obliged to go back to her couch, where she sank into slumber. Alas! Filled as I was with hope, I saw in Atala's weakness only passing signs of weariness!

The next day I woke to the song of cardinals and mocking birds nesting in the acacias and laurels all about the grotto. I went to pick a magnolia blossom and laid it, moist with the tears of morning, on the head of my sleeping Atala. In keeping with the faith of my land, I hoped that the soul of some child who had died at the breast had descended on this flower in a dewdrop, and that a happy dream would bear it into the bosom of my future bride. Then I sought out my host. I found him with his robe tucked up into his two pockets and a rosary in his hand, sitting and waiting for me on the trunk of a pine tree which had fallen with age. He invited me to go with him to the mission, while Atala still lay resting. I accepted his suggestion, and we set forth at once.

Going down the mountain I observed some oak trees where the spirits seemed to have cut strange characters. The hermit told me that he had carved them himself, and that they were verses of an ancient poet, named Homer, and a few maxims of an even more ancient poet, called Solomon. There was a strange and mysterious harmony between this wisdom of the ages, these verses overgrown by moss, this old hermit who had engraved them, and these aged oak trees which served as his books.

His name, his age, and the date of his mission were also marked on a reed of the savannah at the foot of these trees. I was astonished at the frailty of this last monument, but the priest observed, "It will endure even longer than I, and it will surely be of more value than the little good which I have done."

Going on, we reached the entrance to a valley, where I beheld a wonderful creation—a natural bridge, like the one in Virginia, of which you may have heard. My son, men, especially those of your country, frequently imitate Nature, and their copies are always petty. It is not so with Nature when she seems to imitate the works of men, while actually offering them models. At such times she hurls bridges from the summit of one mountain to the summit of the next, suspends roads in the clouds, spreads rivers for canals, carves mountains for columns, and for pools she hollows out seas.

As we passed under the single arch of this bridge, we

found ourselves before another wonder, the cemetery of the mission Indians or the Groves of Death. Father Aubry had allowed his converts to bury their dead in their own manner and preserve their Indian name for the place of their burials; he had merely hallowed the spot with a cross. The ground was divided, like the community harvest field, into as many lots as there were families. Each lot was in itself a clump of woods varying with the taste of those who had planted it. A stream wound silently among these groves, and it was known as the Stream of Peace. This lovely refuge for souls was bounded on the east by the bridge under which we had passed, and two hills enclosed it on the north and south; only in the west did it open out to a great forest of pine trees. The trunks of these trees were red streaked with green, and rose without branches to their tops, resembling lofty columns which formed the peristyle of this temple of death. The atmosphere was permeated with a religious resonance like the muffled roar of the organ beneath the vaults of a church. But within the depths of the sanctuary, nothing could be heard but the hymn of the birds glorifying the memory of the dead in eternal celebration.

As we emerged from this forest the mission village appeared, situated on the shore of a lake in the midst of a flower-strewn savannah. The approach led through an avenue of magnolias and live oaks bordering one of the ancient roads near the mountains between Kentucky and the Floridas. No sooner had the Indians caught sight of their pastor in the plain than they abandoned their tasks and hastened out to meet him. Some kissed his robe, others helped him as he walked. Mothers raised their little children in their arms to show them the man of Christ, while he, in turn, shed tears. As he walked along he inquired about all that was going on in the village; to one he gave advice, another he gently rebuked; he spoke of gathering in the harvests, of teaching the young and consoling the suffering, and in all his conversations he spoke about God.

Escorted in this manner we reached the foot of a great

cross set up beside the road. It was here that the servant of God was wont to celebrate the mysteries of his religion. "Dear Christians," he said turning to the assemblage, "a brother and a sister have come among you, and to crown your good fortune, I see that Divine Providence yesterday spared your harvests; here are two great reasons to render Him thanks. Let us, therefore, offer up the holy sacrifice, and let each of you bring to it profound meditation, living faith, infinite gratitude, and a humble heart."

Immediately the holy priest donned a white tunic of mulberry bark, the sacred vessels were taken forth from a tabernacle at the foot of the cross, the altar was prepared on a section of a rock, water was drawn from the near-by stream, and a cluster of wild grapes supplied the wine for the sacrifice. We fell to our knees in the tall grass, and the divine mystery began.

The new day appearing behind the mountains was setting the east ablaze. Everywhere the solitude was bathed in golden hues and rose. The great star heralded with such splendor finally came forth from a vastness of light, and its first ray fell upon the consecrated host, which the priest at that moment was lifting in the air. O joy of religion! O magnificence of Christian worship! For a celebrant an old hermit, for an altar a rock, for a church the wilderness, and for a congregation innocent savages! No, I cannot doubt that the great mystery was fulfilled when we prostrated ourselves, and that God descended to earth, for I felt Him descend in my heart.

After the sacrifice, during which I missed only the daughter of Lopez, we went on to the village. There the most charming harmony of social and natural life prevailed. In a corner of a cypress grove, in what had once been the wilderness, new cultivation was coming to life. Ears of grain were swaying in golden billows over the trunk of a fallen oak, and the sheaf of a summer replaced the tree of three centuries. Everywhere the forests were delivered to the flames and sending dense clouds of smoke up in the air,

while the plow went its slow way among the remains of
their roots. Surveyors with long chains went about measuring the land. Arbitrators were establishing the first properties. The bird surrendered its nest, and the lair of the wild
beast was changing to a cabin. Forges were heard rumbling,
and the falling axe was forcing the last groans from the
echoes as they expired with the trees which had served as
their refuge.

I wandered in delight amid these scenes, and they grew
even lovelier with the thought of Atala and the dreams of
joy gladdening my heart. I marveled at the triumph of
Christianity over primitive culture. I could see the Indian
growing civilized through the voice of religion. I was witnessing the primal wedding of man and the earth, with man
delivering to the earth the heritage of his sweat, and the
earth, in return, undertaking to bear faithfully man's harvests, his sons and his ashes.

Meanwhile a child was held out to the missionary to receive baptism among the flowering jasmine by the edge of a
brook, while a coffin moved along amidst children's games
and adult labors to the Groves of Death. A young couple
received the wedding benediction beneath an oak, and then
we went along to settle them in a corner of the wilderness.
The pastor walked before us, blessing as he went the rock,
the tree, and the spring, just as long ago, according to the
book of the Christians, God blessed the virgin earth as
He gave it to Adam for a heritage. As I watched this procession trooping along with its flocks from rock to rock behind
its venerable leader, my heart was touched deeply, and I
recalled the migrations of the first families, in the days when
Shem was making his way with his children through an unknown world, following the sun which advanced before him.

I was anxious to learn from the saintly hermit how he
governed his children. He replied with deep kindness: "I
have given them no law. I have taught them only to love
one another, to pray to God, and look forward to a better
life, for in these simple teachings are all the world's laws.

In the middle of the village you will see a cabin somewhat larger than the rest; it serves as a chapel in the rainy season. There we gather morning and night to praise the Lord, and when I am not there, an old man performs the service, for age, like motherhood, confers a kind of priesthood. Then we go off to labor in the fields, and although properties are divided, in order that all may learn to live in organized society, the harvests are placed in community granaries, and thus we may all practice brotherly charity. Four elders distribute equally the fruits of the farming. Add to this our religious ceremonies, a great many hymns, the cross where I celebrate the mysteries, the elm beneath which I preach on fair days, our graves close beside our corn fields, our rivers where I immerse little children and the Saint Johns of this new Bethany, and you will have a complete idea of this kingdom of Christ."

These words of the recluse delighted my heart, and I felt the superiority of this stable, busy life over the savage's idle wandering.

Ah! René, surely I will not murmur against Providence, yet I confess that I never recall that evangelical society without feeling bitter pangs of regret. How joyous my life had been could I have settled with Atala in a hut by those shores! There all my wanderings would have come to an end; there together with my bride and unknown to men, concealing my happiness in the heart of the forest, I would have passed by like the nameless rivers in the wilderness. But instead of this peace which I dared to expect, what anguish has weighed down my days! To become the perpetual plaything of fortune, dashed against every strand, long exiled from my country, and finding on my return only a cabin in ruins and friends in the grave—such was to be the fate of Chactas.

The Drama

My dream of happiness, vivid though it was, was short-lived, and a brusque awakening was in store for me at the hermit's grotto. As we approached it in the middle of the day, I was surprised not to see Atala hasten out to greet us. A strange terror suddenly gripped me. We drew near the cave, but I dared not call out to Atala, for my imagination dreaded both the sounds or the silence which would answer my cry. Frightened even more by the darkness in the entrance to the rock, I said to the missionary: "You, whom Heaven sustains and strengthens, go in among those shadows."

How weak he is whom passions buffet, how strong the man who rests in God! There was more courage in that religious heart, withered by its seventy-six years, than in all my ardent youth. The man of peace went into the grotto, while I remained without, mortally afraid. Soon a feeble murmur, which sounded like a moan, reached my ear from the depths of the rock. With a shriek I found my strength again, and plunged into the somber cave. O spirit of my fathers, you alone know what sight struck my eyes!

The hermit had lit a pine torch, and was holding it in his trembling hand over Atala's couch. The beautiful young woman was half raised on her elbow, pale and disheveled. Beads of painladen sweat glistened on her brow. Her dull eyes still sought to express her love for me, and her mouth attempted a smile. Transfixed as though by a thunderbolt, my eyes staring, my arms outstretched, and my lips apart, I stood motionless. For a moment deep silence enveloped the three characters in that sorrowful scene. The hermit was first to break it: "This is probably nothing more than a fever caused by fatigue," he said. "If we resign ourselves to God's will, He will take pity on us."

At these words, the blood which had frozen in my heart began to flow again, and, with the savage's agility, I swung suddenly from extreme fear to extreme confidence. But Atala soon left me little hope. Sadly shaking her head, she beckoned to us to draw near her couch.

"Father," she said, weakly addressing the holy man, "I am on the verge of death. O Chactas! Do not despair and listen to the fatal secret which I have hidden from you only because I wished to preserve you from sorrow and obey my mother. Try not to interrupt me with signs of your grief, for they would shorten the few moments I still have to live. I have many things to tell, and by these faltering beats of my heart—by some strange, icy weight which my breast can barely lift—I feel that I must speak quickly."

After a few moments of silence, Atala went on.

"My sad fate began almost before I saw the light of day. My mother had conceived me in grief; I was a burden to her womb, and I came into the world sharply rending her body. My life was given up for lost, and to save me from death, my mother vowed to the Queen of Angels that, if I were spared, my virginity would be consecrated to her. That was the fatal vow which is now forcing me to my grave!

"I was beginning my sixteenth year when I lost my mother. A few hours before her death, she called me to her bedside, where a missionary was consoling her in her last moments. 'My daughter,' she said, 'you know about the vow I once made for you. Would you have your mother speak falsely? O my Atala! I leave you in a world unworthy of having a Christian woman in the midst of heathens who persecute your father's God and mine, the God who first gave you life and then preserved it by a miracle. Ah, my dear child, when you accept the virgin's veil, you give up only the cares of the cabin and the mortal passions which distressed your mother's bosom. Come, then, beloved daughter, swear upon this image of the Savior's mother, under the hands of the holy priest and before your dying mother, that you will not betray me in the face of Heaven. Remember that I gave my word for you in order to save your life, and if you do not keep my promise, you will plunge your mother's soul into everlasting woe.'

"O mother! Why did you speak thus? O religion, at once my sadness and my joy, my doom and consolation! And you, dear sad friend, for whom I am consumed with passion even in the arms of death, O Chactas, you see now what has made our fate so grim!

"Bursting into tears and throwing myself upon my mother's bosom, I promised to do everything I was asked to do. Then the missionary pronounced the terrible words over me and gave me the scapulary which binds me forever. My mother threatened me with her curse if ever I broke my vows; then exhorting me to keep my secret secure from the heathens who persecute my religion, she died with her arms enfolding me.

"At first I was not aware of the danger of my oath. Being full of fervor and genuinely Christian, and proud of the Spanish blood coursing through my veins, I saw all about me only men unworthy of receiving my hand. I took pride in having no husband other than the God of my mother. I laid eyes on you, handsome young captive, I was stirred by your fate, I ventured to speak to you at the stake in the forest—and then I felt the full weight of my vows."

As Atala's last words died away, I clenched my fists and glared at the missionary with a menacing expression. "So this is the religion you vaunt so highly," I cried. "A curse on the oath which robs me of Atala! Death to the God who chokes off nature! Priest man, why did you ever come to these forests?"

"To save you," said the old man in a terrible voice, "to subdue your passions and prevent you, blasphemer, from drawing down on your head the wrath of Heaven! Truly it behooves you to complain of your sorrows, frail young man hardly out of your cradle! Where are the marks of your suffering? Where are the injustices you have borne? Where are your virtues which alone could give you some right to complain? What service have you rendered? What good have you done? Ah, miserable creature! You offer me but your passions, and you dare censure Heaven! When you have spent thirty years in exile on the mountains, like Father Aubry, you will be less quick to judge the purposes of Providence. You will understand then that you know nothing, that you are nothing, and that there is no punishment, however severe, no suffering, however terrible, which the corrupt flesh does not deserve to suffer."

The fire flashing from the old man's eyes, his beard beating against his breast, and his terrifying words made him very like a god. Crushed by his majesty, I fell at his knees and asked him to forgive me for my violent outburst. "My son," he replied in so gentle a tone that remorse stole into my soul, "it was not for myself that I rebuked you. Alas, you are right, my dear child. I have done little indeed in these forests, and God has no servant more unworthy than I. But, my son, it is Heaven, Heaven, which you must never condemn! Forgive me if I have wounded you, and let us listen now to your sister. There may still be some remedy; let us never tire of hoping. Chactas, it is a truly divine faith which has made a virtue of hope!"

"My young friend," continued Atala, "you have witnessed my struggle, and yet you have seen but a small part of it; the rest I carefully concealed. No, the black slave who soaks the burning sands of Florida with his sweat is less wretched than was I. I exhorted you to escape, though I was certain of death if we parted; I was afraid to flee with you to the wilderness, yet I panted with desire for the shade of the woods. Ah, if I had only had to leave my relatives and friends and country; if even—oh, dreadful thought!—I could have suffered only the loss of my soul! But your shade, O mother, your shade was ever present, reproaching me with its torments! I kept hearing your moans, I saw you devoured in the flames of hell. My nights were arid and filled with phantoms, my days were desolate. The evening dew dried as it touched my burning skin. I parted my lips to the breeze, and the breeze, far from cooling them, caught fire from the heat of my breath. What torture to see you constantly by my side, far from all men in deepest solitude, and to feel between us an invincible barrier! To spend my life at your feet and wait on you as a slave, preparing your table and couch in some unknown corner of the universe—this would have been my supreme happiness; such happiness was within reach, and I could not attain it.

"What plans I treasured! What dreams came from my saddened heart! Sometimes, as I fixed my eyes upon you, my desires would go to the wildest and most forbidden extremes. I wanted to be the only living creature on earth with you; or else, feeling some divinity restraining me in my dreadful ecstasies, I longed for the annihilation of the divinity, if only, clasped in your arms, I could plunge through endless depths along with the ruins of God and the universe! Even now—dare I say this!—now that eternity is about to engulf me and I am going to appear before the inexorable Judge, at this very moment when, to obey my mother, I joyfully see my chastity consuming my life—well, by some horrible contradiction, I bear away remorse for not having been yours! . . ."

"My daughter," interrupted the missionary, "you are distraught by your suffering. This extreme passion to which you surrender is seldom right; it is not even natural, and therefore it is less guilty in the eyes of God, because it is an error of the mind, rather than a vice of the heart. You must give up these intense emotions which are unworthy of your innocence. Besides, my dear child, your impulsive imagination has given you needless alarm about your vows. Religion does not exact superhuman sacrifices. Its genuine feelings and temperate virtues are far loftier than the impassioned feelings and extreme virtues of so-called heroism. Even if you had succumbed, poor lamb gone astray, well, the Good Shepherd would have sought you out and brought you back to the flock. The treasures of repentance were open to you. Only rivers of blood can rub out our sins in the eyes of men; but for God a single tear is enough. Take heart, then, my

dear daughter, your situation requires calm. Let us turn to
God, who heals all the afflictions of His servants. If, as I
hope, it is His will that you recover from this illness, I shall
write to the Bishop of Quebec; he has the power to absolve
you of your vows which are not permanently binding, and
you will end your days beside me with Chactas as your
husband."

As the old man finished speaking, Atala was overcome by
a long convulsion, followed by signs of horrible suffering.
"What," she said, clasping her hands passionately, "there
was a solution? I could have been absolved of my vows?"
"Yes, my daughter," replied the priest, "and there is still
time." "It is too late, too late!" she cried. "Must I die the
very moment I learn I might have been happy? Oh, that I
had known this saintly old man sooner! What happiness I
could be enjoying today, Chactas, with you as a Christian,
and I comforted and encouraged by this venerable priest—
in the wilderness—forever—oh! it would have been too
joyous!" "Be calm," I said, taking the hapless girl's hand,
"be calm, and we shall yet taste of that happiness." "Never!
never!" said Atala. "What?" I uttered with growing anxiety.
"You do not know all," she cried. "It was yesterday—during
the storm. I was about to break my vow. I was about to hurl
my mother into the flames of damnation. Already her curse
was upon me, already I was being false to the God who had
saved my life. When you were kissing my trembling lips, you
did not know that you were embracing death!" "O heaven,"
cried the missionary, "dear child, what have you done?" "It
was a crime, father," said Atala with a haggard look, "but I
was destroying myself alone and saving my mother." "Tell
me everything," I cried out in terror. "Well!" she said then,
"I foresaw my weakness; and when I left the cabins, I took
along with me . . ." "What?" I breathed in horrified suspense. "Poison?" asked the father. "It is now in my breast,"
cried Atala.

The torch dropped away from the hermit's hand, and I
fell in a dead faint beside the daughter of Lopez. The old

man took both of us in his arms, and together, in the darkness over the death bed, we mingled our sobs.

"We must awake, we must awake!" said the brave hermit at length, lighting up a lamp. "We are wasting precious moments. Let us face the onslaughts of adversity as fearless Christians. With ropes around our necks and ashes on our heads, let us throw ourselves at the feet of the Almighty, imploring His mercy and submitting to His decrees. There may yet be time. My daughter, you should have warned me last night."

"Alas! father," said Atala, "I looked for you in the night but, to punish me for my sins, Heaven took you away from me. Besides, all help would have been futile, for the Indians themselves, with all their skill in poisons, know of no antidote for the one I have taken. O Chactas! Imagine my feelings when I saw that the end did not come as suddenly as I had expected! Love multiplied my strength, and my soul refused to be parted from you so soon."

And now it was no longer with my sobs that I disturbed Atala's tale, but with bursts of frenzied fury known only to savages. I went rolling wildly over the ground, twisting my arms and biting my hands. The old priest, with marvelous tenderness, hurried between brother and sister, lavishing on us infinite care. Through the calm of his heart and the burden of his years, he could speak to us in our youth so that we could understand, and his faith lent him accents even more tender and burning than our own passions. In his forty years of daily devotion to God and men on the mountain, does not this priest call to mind those awesome burnt offerings of Israel, perpetually smoking in high places before the lord?

Alas! It was in vain that he tried to bring succor for Atala's anguish. Fatigue, sorrow, poison, and a passion more deadly than all poisons together were combining to spirit this flower away from our solitude. As evening drew near, terrifying symptoms set in. Spreading numbness gripped Atala's limbs, and her hands and feet began to grow cold.

"Touch my fingers," she said to me. "Are they not quite chilled?" I could not answer, and my hair began bristling with horror. Then she went on: "Only yesterday, my beloved, the thrill of your touch still made me quiver, and now I cannot feel your hand any more, I can barely hear your voice, the objects in the grotto are vanishing one by one. Are those not birds singing? The sun must be close to setting now; Chactas, how beautifully its rays will shine in the wilderness on my grave!"

Perceiving that these words were bringing tears to our eyes, Atala said to us: "Forgive me, kind friends, I am weak indeed, but I shall perhaps grow stronger. And yet, to die so young, so suddenly, when my heart is so full of life! Leader in prayer, have pity on me, and sustain me. Do you think my mother will be content and God will forgive me for what I have done?"

"My daughter," replied the gentle priest wiping away his tears with a trembling, mutilated hand, "all your sorrows are born of ignorance. It was your primitive education and the lack of necessary teaching which brought on this calamity. You did not know that a Christian may not dispose of his life as he wishes. Take solace, then, beloved lamb, God will forgive you because of your heart's innocence. Your mother and the rash missionary who guided her were more guilty than you. They went beyond their powers in forcing from you an unwise vow. But the Lord's peace be with them! All three of you offer a terrible example of the dangers of passion and the want of light in religious matters. Be calm, my child, men's bodies and hearts hold no mystery for God; He will judge you for your intention, which was pure, and not for your action, which was guilty.

"As for your mortal life, if the moment has come for you to sleep in the Lord, ah, my dear child, how little you lose in losing this world! Although you have lived in solitude, you have known sorrow; what would you have thought had you witnessed the evils of society, had your ears been assailed, as you set foot on Europe's shores, by the long cry of woe rising out of that ancient land? The hut dweller and the palace lord both suffer alike, and all lament together in this world. Queens have been seen weeping like simple women, and men have stood aghast at the volume of tears in the eyes of kings!

"Is it your love you regret losing? My daughter, you might as well weep over a dream. Do you understand the heart of man, and could you count his changing desires? It would be simpler to add up the waves tossed about in a tempestuous sea. Atala, sacrifices and kindness are not eternal bonds. One day, perhaps, disgust would have set in with satiety, the past would have counted as nothing, and you would have felt only the vexations of an impoverished and despised union. My daughter, the most beautiful love of all was doubtless that of the man and woman formed by the hand of the Creator. A paradise had been fashioned out for them, and they were innocent and immortal. Perfect in soul and in body they harmonized in everything. Eve had been created for Adam, and Adam for Eve. If they were unable to abide in that happy state, what couple after them will ever be able to do so? I will not mention those marriages of the first-born of men, those unutterable unions, when the sister was wife to the brother, when love and brotherly affection were blended in the same heart and the purity of one swelled the delight of the other. All those unions were troubled. Jealousy crept toward the grass altar upon which the kid was sacrificed, it dwelt beneath the tent of Abraham and even over those couches where the patriarchs enjoyed such bliss as to forget the death of their mothers.

"Could you have presumed, then, my child, to be happier and more innocent in your ties than those holy families from which Christ chose to descend? I shall spare you the details of the household cares, the quarrels, the mutual reproaches, the anxieties, and all those secret sorrows which lie heavy on the pillow of the marriage bed. Woman marries in tears, and renews her suffering each time she becomes a mother. What grief alone in the loss of a new-born child who has drunk its

mother's milk and died on her breast! The mountain echoed
with lamentation, and Rachel would not be consoled when
her sons were no more. The bitterness underlying human
affections is so strong that in my native land I have seen great
ladies, beloved of kings, leave the court and vanish into
cloisters, there to mutilate the unsubdued flesh whose
pleasures are so painful.

"Perhaps you feel that those circumstances were different,
and that your entire ambition was simply to live in a humble
cabin with the man of your choosing, and not to seek the
sweetness of marriage so much as that intriguing madness
which youth calls 'love.' All illusion, all foolish fantasy, the
vanity and dream of a wounded imagination! I too, my
daughter, have known the heart's turmoils; this head you
see was not always bald nor this breast so calm as it seems
today. Trust my experience; if man were ever constant in
his affections, if his feelings remained eternally fresh and he
could strengthen them endlessly, then solitude and love
would surely make him God's equal, for those are the Great
Being's two eternal pleasures. But man's soul grows weary,
and never for long does it lavish its love on the same object.
Invariably there are places where two hearts do not touch,
and in the end those places are enough to make life unbearable.

"And lastly, my dear daughter, the great mistake of men,
in their vision of happiness, is to forget the frailty inherent
in their nature—they must one day die. Sooner or later,
whatever had been your bliss, those fine features would have
turned to the uniform mask which the sepulchre gives to
the whole family of Adam. The eye of Chactas himself could
not have distinguished you from your sisters in the grave.
Love has no sway over the worms in the coffin. What is this
I am saying!—O vanity of vanities!—Why do I say anything
of the power of earthly affections? My dear daughter, shall I
tell you how deeply they go? If a man were to return to this
sphere several years after his death, I doubt that he would be
received joyfully by the very persons who had shed the most

tears for his memory, so quickly do we form other ties, so easily do we adopt other habits, so natural is man's infidelity, so trivial a thing is our life even in the hearts of our friends!

"Be grateful, then, to Providence, my dear daughter, for bearing you off so soon from this vale of tears. Already the white raiment and dazzling crown of virgins are being prepared for you on high. Already I hear the Queen of Angels calling to you: 'Come, my worthy servant, come, my fair dove, come and take your place on a throne of candor, amongst all those maidens who have sacrificed their youth and beauty to the service of humanity, to the education of children and to great works of penitence. Come, mystic rose, come and lie down on the bosom of Jesus. The sepulture which you have chosen for your nuptial bed will never be dishonored, and the embraces of your heavenly spouse will never end!' "

As the last blush of day stills the wind and spreads peace through the heavens, so the old man's calm words soothed the passions in my beloved's breast. She now seemed concerned only with my sorrow and sought only to help me endure my loss. She said she would die happy if only I promised to wipe away my tears; then she spoke of my mother and my native land, trying to distract me from my present sorrow by reviving in me a sorrow of the past. She implored me to have patience and courage. "You will not always be sad," she said. "Heaven may be trying you today, but it is only to make you compassionate for the sorrows of others. The human heart, O Chactas, is like those trees which do not yield their balm for the wounds of men until they themselves have been wounded by the axe."

So saying, she turned toward the missionary, seeking the same solace she had just given me, and thus with her own consolation and the consolation of the hermit, she bestowed and accepted the life-giving word, lying there on her bed of death.

Meanwhile the hermit's zeal was growing apace. His aged bones had kindled anew with the ardor of charity, and as he hastened about preparing remedies, lighting the fire and freshening the couch, he uttered wonderful thoughts about God and the joy of the righteous. With the torch of faith in his hand he seemed to usher Atala into the grave to reveal to her its awesome mysteries. The humble grotto was permeated with the grandeur of this Christian demise, and the heavenly spirits were surely watching this scene where faith struggled single-handed against love, youth, and death.

And that holy faith was indeed conquering; we could observe its victory as a reverent sadness settled into our hearts after the first transports of passion. Toward the middle of the night Atala seemed to revive and was able to repeat prayers which the missionary recited at her bedside. A little while later she held out her hand to me whispering in a barely audible voice: "Son of Outalissi, do you remember that first night when you took me for the Maiden of Last Love? What a strange omen of our fate!" She paused and went on: "When I reflect that I am about to leave you forever, my heart makes such desperate efforts to return to life that I feel within me the power to become immortal by the sheer force of my love. But, O God, Thy will be done!" Atala was silent a few moments, and then added: "All that remains for me now is to ask you to forgive me for the grief I have brought you. I have troubled you deeply with my pride and my whims. Chactas, the handful of earth you will throw on my body will soon place a whole world between us and will deliver you forever from the burden of my misfortunes."

"Forgive you!" I gasped out, bathed in tears. "Was it not I who brought about all your sorrows?" "Dear friend," she interrupted, "you have made me infinitely happy, and if I were to begin life anew, I would still prefer the joy of loving you a few moments in the hardship of exile to a whole life of repose in my native land."

Here Atala's voice faded away. The shadows of death crept slowly round her eyes and mouth. Her groping fingers sought to touch something, and she was whispering with unseen spirits. Soon, with an effort, she tried to detach the

little crucifix from her throat, but her effort was futile, and
she begged me to untie it myself; then she said:

"When I spoke to you the first time by the light of the fire,
you saw this cross glittering on my breast; it is my only possession. Lopez, your father and mine, sent it to my mother a
few days after my birth. Take this heritage from me, O my
brother, and keep it in memory of my sorrows. In the trials
of your life, you will yet have recourse to the God of the
unfortunate. Chactas, I have one last request to make of you.
Dear friend, our union on earth could only have been short,
but there is after this life a longer life. How terrible it would
be to be separated from you forever! Today I am only going
on before you, and I shall wait for you in the celestial realm.
If you have loved me, learn the lessons of the Christian faith,
and it will prepare our reunion. It is performing a miracle
before your eyes, since it gives me strength to leave you without dying in the throes of despair. And yet, Chactas, all I ask
of you is a simple promise, for I know only too well the price
of an oath. Perhaps a vow would separate you from some
more fortunate woman than I; O mother! Forgive your
daughter; O Virgin! Contain thy wrath. I am slipping back
into my weaknesses and robbing Thee, O my God, of
thoughts which should be Thine alone."

Crushed with sorrow, I promised Atala that I would one
day embrace the Christian faith. Seeing such a scene, the
hermit rose with an inspired air and lifted his arms to the
vault of the grotto. "It is time," he cried, "time to summon
God hither."

Scarcely had he pronounced these words when a supernatural power forced me to my knees and bowed my head
down at the foot of Atala's bed. The priest opened a hidden
compartment containing a golden vase covered with a silken
veil. He bent low and worshiped fervently. Suddenly the
grotto appeared illuminated; voices of angels and trembling
notes of heavenly harps were heard in the air, and when the
hermit drew the sacred vessel from his tabernacle, I thought
I saw God Himself emerging from the mountainside.

Uncovering the chalice the priest took the snow-white host between his two fingers and drew near Atala, pronouncing all the while mysterious words. The eyes of the saintly maid were lifted ecstatically to heaven. All her sorrows seemed suspended and all her vital force was centered at her mouth. Her lips parted and came forward reverently to meet the God concealed in the mystical bread. Then the holy patriarch dipped a piece of cotton into consecrated oil and anointed Atala's temples; for a moment he watched the dying girl, and then suddenly from his lips sprang these powerful words: "Depart, Christian soul, go forth and rejoin thy Creator!" Raising my lowered head, I cried out as I looked at the vessel with the holy oil: "Father, will this remedy restore Atala to life?" "Yes, my son," said the old man falling into my arms, "to life eternal!" Atala had just breathed her last.

At this point, for the second time since the beginning of his story, Chactas was obliged to interrupt himself. His tears overwhelmed him, and from his lips came only broken words. The blind sachem searched in his breast and drew out Atala's crucifix. "Here is this token of adversity," he cried. "O René, O my son! You can see it, but I no longer can! Tell me, is not the gold dulled after so many years, and can you not discern the trace my tears have left upon it? Could you recognize the spot where a saintly woman's lips once touched it? How can it be that I am still not a Christian? What petty motives of politics and patriotism have kept me in the errors of my fathers? No, I will not delay any longer. The earth cries out to me: 'When will you come down to your grave, and why do you still hesitate to embrace a divine faith?' O earth! You shall not long wait for me. As soon as a priest has restored youth with holy waters to this head now whitened by trials, I hope to find Atala again. But let me finish what still remains of my story.

The Funeral

I shall not attempt to portray for you, O René, the despair which gripped my soul when Atala had uttered her last sigh. I would need greater fervor than I have left, and my closed eyes would have to open again and ask the sun for an accounting of the tears they have shed by its light. Yes, that moon now shining overhead will grow weary of lighting up the solitudes of Kentucky, and the river now bearing our pirogues along will stay the flow of its waters before my tears for Atala dry up! For two whole days I was numb to the hermit's words. In his efforts to allay my grief the excellent man never used the hollow persuasions of the world; he merely said, "My son, it is God's will," and he clasped me in his arms. Had I not experienced it myself, I would never have believed there could be so much consolation in those few words of a Christian resigned to fate.

The tenderness, the earnestness, and the untiring patience of the old servant of God finally subdued my stubborn sorrow. I was ashamed of the tears he kept shedding for me. "Father," I said, "I have gone too far; the passions of a young man must no longer disturb the peace of your days. Let me only bear away with me the remains of my bride. I shall bury them in some corner of the wilderness, and if I am still condemned to live, I shall endeavor to grow worthy of the eternal wedding promised me by Atala."

At this unhoped-for rebirth of courage, the good father started with joy. "O blood of Christ," he cried, "blood of my divine Master, in this I recognize Thy virtue! Surely Thou wilt save this youth. Dear God! Fulfill Thy work; restore peace in this troubled soul, and leave with him only humble and useful memories of his sorrows!"

The righteous man refused to give up Atala's body, but proposed instead to summon his converts and bury her with full Christian solemnity. This I in turn refused. "Atala's sorrows and virtues were unknown to men," I said. "Her grave must be dug out in secrecy by our own hands and must share in that obscurity." We agreed to set out the next day at sunrise and bury Atala beneath the arch of the natural bridge at the entrance to the Groves of Death. We resolved also to spend the night in prayer beside the body of the saintly maid.

Toward evening we took up the precious remains and brought them to an opening of the grotto facing northward. The hermit had wrapped them in a piece of European linen, which had been spun by his mother; it was the only possession he still had from his native land, and he had long intended it for his own tomb. Atala lay on a carpet of mountain mimosa. Her feet, her head and shoulders, and part of her breast were uncovered. In her hair was a withered magnolia blossom—the very one I had laid on the maiden's bed to foster her fertility. Her lips, like a rose bud picked two mornings before, seemed to languish and smile wanly. In her dazzling white cheeks blue veins were visible. Her fine eyes were closed and her modest feet together, while her alabaster hands pressed to her heart an ebony cross. Suspended from her neck was the scapulary of her vows. She seemed enchanted by the Angel of Melancholy and by the twofold slumber of innocence and death. Never have I laid eyes on anything more heavenly. Whoever was unaware that this maid had once enjoyed the light of day might have taken her for a statue of sleeping virginity.

The holy man never ceased praying all night, while I sat silently at the head of my Atala's funeral bed. How often had I held her lovely head on my knees while she slept! How often had I leaned over to hear her breathing and inhale her fragrance! But now no sound emerged from that motionless breast, and I waited in vain for the beauteous creature to awake!

The moon lent its pale torch for this funeral vigil. It rose in the middle of the night, like a white-robed vestal coming

to weep over the bier of a companion. Soon it spread through
the woods that vast melancholy secret which it loves to tell to
the old oak trees and the ancient shores of the sea. From time
to time the priest dipped a blossoming twig into consecrated
water, and, waving the wet branch, perfumed the night with
heavenly redolence. Now and then he would chant to an
age-old melody some verses of an ancient poet named Job.

"I have passed away like a flower; I am withered as the
grass of the fields.

"Wherefore is light given to him that is in misery, and life
unto the bitter in soul?"

Thus sang the ancient among men. His grave, unrhyth-
mical voice reverberated out into the silence of the wilderness, and the name of God and the tomb echoed back from
all the waters and all the forests. The cooing of the Virginia
dove, the falling of the mountain torrent and the tolling of
the bell to summon wayfarers, all mingled with these funeral
chants, while from the Groves of Death the far-away choir
of the departed could almost be heard replying to the voice
of the hermit.

Meanwhile a golden stripe was forming in the east. Spar-
row hawks were calling from the rocks, and martens were
retiring to the hollows of the elms; it was the signal for
Atala's funeral procession. I lifted the body to my shoulders,
and the hermit went before me with a spade in his hand. We
began the descent from rock to rock, with old age and death
both slowing our pace. At the sight of the dog who had
found us in the forest, and who now, still leaping with joy,
guided us along a very different path, I burst into tears.
Many times as the morning breeze played through Atala's
long tresses, a golden veil was spread before my eyes; often,
too, I sagged beneath my burden and was obliged to set it
down on the moss and rest beside it to recover my strength.
At last we reached the spot marked out by my sorrow and
went down under the arch of the bridge. O my son! Picture
a young Indian and an old hermit kneeling opposite one
another and using their hands to dig a grave for a poor girl

whose body lay near by, in a ravine where the stream had run dry.

When our work was done we carried the beautiful one to her earthen bed. Alas! It was another couch I had hoped to prepare for her! In terrible silence, I took up a little dust in my hand and fixed my eyes for the last time on Atala's countenance. Then I scattered the earth of sleep on a brow of eighteen springtimes and watched my sister's features gradually disappear as the curtain of eternity enveloped her graces. For a little while yet her breast rose above the black soil, as a white lily rises out of dark earth. "Lopez," I cried out, "behold your son interring your daughter!" and I finished covering Atala with the earth of everlasting sleep.

We returned to the grotto, and I told the missionary that I planned to settle down near him. The saint, who had a wondrous understanding of the heart of man, soon penetrated my thought and the artfulness of my sorrow. He said to me: "Chactas, son of Outalissi, while Atala still lived I urged you myself to dwell here beside me, but now your lot is changed; you owe your life to your country. Believe me, my son, sorrows are not eternal. Sooner or later they must come to an end, because the heart of man is finite—this is one of our great miseries. We cannot even be unhappy for long. Return to the Meschacebe. Go back and console your mother, who weeps for you daily and needs your support. When you have the occasion, learn about your Atala's religion and remember that you promised her to be virtuous and Christian. As for me, I shall keep vigil here over her grave. Go, my son, and God, your sister's soul, and your old friend's heart will go with you."

Such were the words of the man of the rock, and his authority was too great, his wisdom too profound to be questioned. The very next day I left my venerable host. As he pressed me to his heart he gave me his last counsels, his last blessing, and his last tears. Then I went down to the grave and was surprised to find a little cross standing erect over death, like a mast still visible over a shipwrecked vessel.

I guessed that the hermit had come in the night to pray at the tomb, and this token of affection and faith brought abundant tears to my eyes. I was tempted to open the grave and look once again on my beloved, but a religious fear held me back. I sat down on the freshly turned earth with my elbows on my knees and my head in my hands, and remained sunken in the bitterest revery. O René! It was then for the first time that I reflected seriously on the vanity of our days and the even greater vanity of our designs! Ah, my child! Who has never had such reflections? I am nothing but an aged stag whitened by the winters; my years vie with those of the crow. And still, in spite of all the days heaped on my head, in spite of my long experience with life, I have never yet met a man who has not been disappointed in his dreams of happiness, nor a heart without its secret wound. The heart most serene in appearance is like the natural well of the Alachua savannah; its surface seems calm and pure, but look down in its depths, and you will discern a great crocodile, nourished in the waters of the well.

And so, having seen the sun rise and set in this place of sorrow, the next day, at the stork's first cry, I made ready to leave the holy sepulchre. I left it as I would a starting point from which I was setting out on a course of virtue. Thrice I summoned forth the soul of Atala, and thrice the Spirit of the Wilderness answered my cries beneath the funeral arch. Then I saluted the east and I perceived, far off in the distance among the mountain paths, the hermit wending his way toward the cabin of some unfortunate. Falling on my knees and embracing the grave fervently, I cried: "Sleep in peace in this foreign soil, O maid crushed by misfortune! As a reward for your love, for your exile and death, you will now be abandoned, even by Chactas!" Then, with tears streaming from my eyes, I left Atala and tore myself away from that place, leaving at the foot of nature's monument an even more awesome monument—the humble tomb of virtue.

EPILOGUE

Chactas, son of Outalissi the Natchez, told this story to René the European. Fathers have repeated it to their children, and I, a traveler in far-distant lands, have faithfully set down what I received from the Indians. In this tale I saw a portrayal of the people of the hunt and the people of the plow; of religion, the supreme lawgiver to men; of the perils of religious ignorance and all-consuming fervor set against the light, the charity, and the true spirit of the Gospel; of the struggles of passion and virtue in an innocent soul; and finally I saw the triumph of Christianity over the most ardent feeling and the most terrible fear—love and death.

I was told this story by a Seminole, and I found it highly edifying and surpassingly beautiful, for he had put into it the flower of the wilderness, the grace of the cabin, and a simplicity in describing sorrow which I cannot boast of having preserved. But one thing I still had to learn. I wondered what had become of Father Aubry, and no one could tell me. And I would never have found out, if Providence, which governs all, had not revealed to me what I sought. This is how it happened.

I had wandered over the shores of the Meschacebe which once formed the southern boundary of New France, and I was curious to see the other wonder of this empire, the falls of Niagara, located in the north. I had come fairly close to the cataract, in what was once the country of the Agannonsioni, when one morning, as I was crossing a plain, I caught sight of a woman sitting under a tree, holding a dead child on her knees. As I softly approached the young mother, I heard her saying:

"If you had remained among us, dear child, how gracefully you would have arched the bow! Your arm would have

subdued the raging bear and your fleeting steps would have
vied with the swiftest roe on the mountain top. Spotless
ermine of the rocks, how young you are to have gone away
to the land of souls! How will you be able to live? Your
father is not there to provide for you with his hunting. You
will be cold, and no spirit will bring you skins for your
coverlets. Oh! I must hasten and join you, to sing you my
lullabies and give you my breast."

According to the Indian custom, the woman wished to dry
her son's body on the branches of a tree, so that she might
then take him to the tombs of his fathers. She therefore
stripped her newborn, and breathing a few instants against
his lips, said to him: "Soul of my son, precious soul, once
your father created you with a kiss on my lips. Alas! Mine
are unable to grant you a second birth." Then laying bare
her breast, she clasped the icy remains to herself, and surely
they would have quickened to life in the warmth of her
motherly bosom, had not God reserved to Himself the life-
giving breath.

She arose and her eyes sought a tree on whose branches she
could place her child. She chose a maple with red blossoms,
festooned with garlands of apios, and breathing the softest
perfumes. Bringing the lower bough down with one hand,
she placed the body upon it with the other. Then she re-
leased the branch, which sprang back to its natural position,
bearing with it the relics of innocence in a retreat of fragrant
foliage. Oh, how moving is this Indian custom! I have seen
you in your desolate settings, haughty monuments of the
Crassi and Caesars, and I still prefer those Indian tombs on
high, those blossoming, verdant sepulchres perfumed by the
bee and swaying in the zephyr, where the nightingale builds
its nest and trills its plaintive melody. If the relics of a young
woman have been hung by her lover's hand on the tree of
death, or if the remains of an adored child have been placed
by its mother in the abode of the little birds, then the fascina-
tion is far greater still.

I drew near the woman as she lamented at the foot of the

maple, and, placing my hands on her head, uttered the three
cries of sorrow. Then, following her example without a
word, I took hold of a branch and fanned away the insects
buzzing about the child's body. But I carefully avoided
frightening a dove near by, for I heard the Indian woman
saying: "Dove, if you are not my son's soul which has now
taken flight, you are surely a mother seeking something to
build your nest. Take some of these hairs, for I shall never
again wash them in esquine water; take them and cradle
your little ones, and may the Great Spirit preserve them."
And the mother wept with joy at the stranger's kindness.

As all this was happening, a young man approached.
"Daughter of Celuta," he said, "take down our child. We
shall stay here no longer, for we leave at the first sun." Then
I said, "Brother, I wish you a blue sky, many roes, a beaver
mantle, and hope. Are you not from this wilderness?" "No,"
replied the young man, "we are exiles in search of a homeland." As he said this, the warrior bent his head to his breast
and struck off some flower heads with the end of his bow.
I saw at once that there were tears in the heart of this story
and said nothing. The woman drew her son down from the
branches of the tree and handed him to her husband. Then
I said, "Will you allow me to light your fire this night?" "We
have no cabin," answered the warrior. "If you wish to follow
us, we are camped by the edge of the falls." "I would indeed
like that," I replied, and we went off together.

Soon we reached the edge of the cataract, whose mighty
roar could be heard from afar. It is formed by the Niagara
River, which emerges from Lake Erie and empties into Lake
Ontario; its perpendicular height is one hundred and forty-
four feet. From Lake Erie to the great plunge, the river flows
in a rapid downgrade, and as it reaches the falls, it is not so
much a river as a sea whose torrents surge into the gaping
mouth of a chasm. The cataract is split into two branches,
and bends in the form of a horseshoe. Between the two falls
an island juts out, hollow underneath, and hanging with all
its trees over the chaos of the waves. The mass of water hur-

tling down in the south curves into a vast cylinder, then
straightens into a snowy sheet, sparkling iridescent in the
sunlight. The eastern branch falls in dismal gloom, calling
to mind some downpour of the great flood. A thousand rain-
bows arch and intersect over the abyss. As it strikes the shud-
dering rock, the water bounds back in foaming whirlpools,
which drift up over the forest like the smoke of some vast
conflagration. The scene is ornate with pine and wild walnut trees and rocks carved out in weird shapes. Eagles, drawn
by air currents, spiral down into the depths of the chasm,
and wolverines dangle by their supple tails from the ends of
low-hanging branches, snatching the shattered corpses of
elk and bears out of the abyss.

As I stood marveling at this spectacle in terrified rapture,
the Indian woman and her husband went on. I looked for
them as I followed the river above the falls and soon found
them in a place well suited to their mourning. Along with
some old people, they were lying on the grass beside human
bones wrapped in animal skins. Amazed by all I had seen in
the past few hours, I sat down beside the young mother and
said, "What does all this mean, my sister?" She replied, "My
brother, it is the earth of our homeland and the ashes of our
ancestors following us in our exile." "And how were you
brought to such a plight?" I exclaimed. Then the daughter
of Celuta began: "We are all that remains of the Natchez.
After the French had massacred our nation to avenge their
brothers, those of our people who had escaped the conquer-
ors found a haven among our neighbors, the Chickasaws.
We remained there in peace for a fairly long time. But it is
now seven moons since the whites of Virginia seized our
lands, telling us that they received them from a European
king. We lifted our eyes to heaven and set forth on our trek
through the wilderness, laden with the remains of our forefathers. I gave birth to my child during the march, and my
milk, spoiled with sorrow, soon killed him." So saying, the
young mother wiped her eyes with the locks of her hair. I,
too, was weeping.

Presently, however, I began again: "My sister, let us worship the Great Spirit, for all things come to pass through His will. We are all but wayfarers on earth, and our fathers before us were not otherwise; but there is a place where one day we shall find rest. If I were not afraid of having the loose tongue of the white man, I would ask whether you have heard of Chactas the Natchez." At these words, the Indian woman looked at me and said, "Who has spoken to you of Chactas the Natchez?" I replied, "Wisdom itself has spread his name." Then the woman went on: "I shall tell you what I know, because you have driven the flies away from my son's body and have just spoken goodly words about the Great Spirit. I am the daughter of the daughter of René the European, who was adopted by Chactas as a son. Chactas received baptism, and both he and my luckless grandfather perished in the massacre." "Man passes endlessly from sorrow to sorrow," I said bowing my head. "Perhaps you could also bring me tidings of Father Aubry." "He was no more fortunate than Chactas," said she. "The Cherokees, who are enemies of the French, invaded his mission, guided by the sound of the bell as it rang to succor travelers. Father Aubry could have saved himself, but he refused to abandon his children and remained as an example to encourage them in their death throes. He was subjected to horrible tortures and burned; but not once could they draw from him a single cry reflecting shame on his God or dishonor on his country. Throughout his agony, he never ceased praying for his torturers or commiserating with the victims in their plight. In order to force a sign of weakness from him, the Cherokees dragged to his feet a Christian savage whom they had fearfully mutilated. They were astonished to see the young man fall to his knees and kiss the old hermit's wounds, while the hermit cried out, 'My child, we have been chosen as a spectacle for the angels and for men.' To prevent him from talking, the enraged Indians forced a red-hot iron down his throat. And then, no longer able to be of consolation to men, he yielded up the ghost.

"It is told that the Cherokees, accustomed as they were to seeing Indians suffer stoically, could not help admitting that there was something in the humble courage of Father Aubry which they had never before known, something which went beyond all earthly courage. A number of them were so deeply impressed by his death that they became Christians.

"Several years later, on his return from the white man's land, Chactas learned of the prayer leader's misfortune and went off to gather up his ashes along with those of Atala. He came to the place where the mission had been, but he could scarcely recognize it. The lake had overflowed its shores, and the savannah had turned into a swamp. The natural bridge had collapsed burying Atala's grave and the Groves of Death under its ruins. Chactas wandered about in the vicinity for a long time. He went to see the hermit's grotto and found it full of brambles and raspberry bushes, with a doe suckling its fawn. He sat down on the rock which had served for the death vigil and saw only some feathers fallen from the wing of the bird of passage. As tears welled up in his eyes, the missionary's tame snake came out of the near-by brush, and curled up at his feet. Chactas picked up this faithful friend, who remained alone amidst the ruins, and warmed him in his bosom. The son of Outalissi has told how several times, as night drew near, he thought he could see the shades of Atala and Father Aubry in the haze of the twilight. These visions filled him with religious dread and sad delight.

"After searching vainly for the graves of his sister and the hermit, he was about to take leave, when the doe of the grotto began bounding before him and stopped at the foot of the mission cross. This cross was now partly submerged in water; the wood was overgrown with moss, and the pelican of the wilds liked to perch on its decaying arms. Chactas guessed that the grateful doe had led him to his host's grave. He dug down under the rock which had once served as an altar, and there he found the remains of a man and a woman. He had no doubt that they were those of the priest and the virgin, buried there perhaps by the angels. He wrapped them in bear skins and set out again for his country, carrying with him those precious remains, which rattled over his shoulder like a quiver of death. At night he placed them under his head, and there came to him dreams of goodness and love. O stranger! Here you may contemplate those bones along with those of Chactas himself."

As the Indian woman uttered these final words, I arose, approached the sacred ashes, and prostrated myself silently before them. Then I went off with long strides, exclaiming as I went: "Thus passes all that is good and virtuous and sensitive on earth! Man, thou art but a fleeting vision, a sorrowful dream. Misery is thy essence, and thou art nothing save in the sadness of thy soul and the eternal melancholy of thy thought!"

These meditations weighed on me all through the night. The next morning, at daybreak, my hosts left me. The young warriors led the march and their wives brought up the rear. Those in front were laden with the holy remains, while those in back carried their new-born infants. In the middle, trudging their slow way, came the elders, placed between their ancestors and their posterity, between their memories and their hope, between the lost homeland and the homeland to come. Oh, how bitterly we weep when thus we abandon our native land, when from the top of the hill of exile we look for the last time on the sheltering roof and the stream near the cabin, still flowing sadly through the solitary fields of our homeland!

Hapless Indians whom I have seen wandering in the wildernesses of the New World with the ashes of your ancestors, you who showed me hospitality in the midst of your misery, today I could not return your kindness, for, like you, I wander at the mercy of men, and, less fortunate than you in my exile, I have not brought with me the bones of my fathers!

René

RENÉ

On arriving among the Natchez René was obliged to take a wife in order to conform to the Indian customs; but he did not live with her. His melancholy nature drew him constantly away into the depths of the woods. There he would spend entire days in solitude, a savage among the savages. Aside from Chactas, his foster father, and Father Souël, a missionary at Fort Rosalie, he had given up all fellowship with men. These two elders had acquired a powerful influence over his heart, Chactas, through his kindly indulgence, and Father Souël, on the contrary, through his extreme severity. Since the beaver hunt, when the blind sachem had told his adventures to René, the young man had consistently refused to talk about his own. And yet both Chactas and the missionary keenly desired to know what sorrow had driven this well-born European to the strange decision of retiring into the wildernesses of Louisiana. René had always claimed that he would not tell his story because it was too insignificant, limited as it was to his thoughts and feelings. "As for the circumstance which induced me to leave for America," he added, "that must forever be buried in oblivion."

Thus several years went by, and the two elders were unable to draw his secret from him. One day, however, he received a letter from Europe, through the Office of Foreign Missions, which so increased his sadness that he felt he had to flee even from his old friends. Now more than ever they exhorted him to open his heart to them. And so great was their tact, so gentle their manner, and so deep the respect they commanded, that he finally felt obliged to yield. He therefore set a day to tell them, not the adventures of his life, for he had never had any, but the innermost feelings of his soul.

On the twenty-first day of the month the Indians call the "moon of flowers," René went to the cabin of Chactas. Giving his arm to the sachem, he led him to a spot under a sassafras tree on the bank of the Meschacebe. Soon afterwards Father Souël arrived at the meeting place. Day was breaking. Off on the plain, some distance away, the Natchez village could be seen with its grove of mulberry trees and its cabins which looked like beehives. The French colony and Fort Rosalie were visible on the river bank at the right. Tents, half-built houses, fortresses just begun, hosts of negroes clearing tracts of land, groups of white men and Indians, all offered a striking contrast of social and primitive ways in this limited space. Towards the east, in the background of this setting, the sun was just beginning to show behind the jagged peaks of the Appalachians, which stood forth like azure symbols against the golden reaches of the sky. In the west, the Meschacebe rolled its waves in majestic stillness, forming for the picture a border of indescribable grandeur.

For some time the young man and the missionary stood marveling at this splendid scene and pitying the sachem who could no longer enjoy it. Then Father Souël and Chactas sat down on the grass at the foot of the tree. René took his place between them, hesitated a moment, and then began speaking in the following manner.

As I open my story, I cannot stifle a feeling of shame. The peace in your hearts, respected elders, and the calm of nature all about me make me blush for the disorder and turmoil of my soul.

How you will pity me! How wretched my perpetual anxieties will seem to you! You who have passed through all the hardships of life, what will you think of a young man with neither strength nor moral courage, who finds the source of his torments within himself, and can hardly lament any misfortunes save those he has brought on himself? Alas! Do not condemn him too severely; he has already been harshly punished!

I cost my mother her life as I came into this world and had to be drawn from her womb with an instrument. My father gave his blessing to my brother because he saw in him his elder son; as for me, I was soon abandoned to strange hands and brought up far from my father's roof.

I was spirited in temper and erratic by nature. As I alternated turbulence and joy with silence and sadness, I would gather my young friends around me, then leave them suddenly and go off to sit by myself watching the swift clouds or listening to the rain falling among the leaves.

Each autumn I would return to the family château, off in the midst of the forests, near a lake in a remote province.

I was timid and inhibited in my father's presence, and found freedom and contentment only with my sister Amelia. We were closely bound together by our tender affinities in mood and taste; my sister was only slightly older than I. We loved to climb the hillside together or go sailing on the lake or wander through the woods under the falling leaves, and even now memories of those rambles fill my soul with delight. O illusions of childhood and homeland, can your sweetness ever fade away?

Sometimes we strolled in silence hearkening to the muffled rumbling of the autumn or the crackling of the dry leaves trailing sadly under our feet. In our innocent games we ran after the swallow in the meadows or the rainbow on the storm-swept hills. At other times we would whisper poetry inspired in us by the spectacle of nature. In my youth I courted the Muses. Nothing is more poetic than a heart of sixteen in all the pristine freshness of its passions. The morning of life is like the morning of the day, pure, picturesque, and harmonious.

On Sundays and holidays I often stood in the deep woods as the sound of the distant bell drifted through the trees, calling from the temple to the man of the fields. Leaning against the trunk of an elm, I would listen in rapt silence to the devout tolling. Each tremor of the resounding bronze would waft into my guileless soul the innocence of country

ways, the calm of solitude, the beauty of religion, and the
cherished melancholy of memories out of my early childhood! Oh! What churlish heart has never started at the
sound of the bells in his birthplace, those bells which trembled with joy over his cradle, which rang out the dawn of
his life, which signaled his first heartbeat, announcing to all
surrounding places the reverent gladness of his father, the
ineffable anguish and supreme joy of his mother! All is embraced in that magical revery which engulfs us at the sound
of our native bell—faith, family, homeland, the cradle and
the grave, the past and the future.

True enough, Amelia and I enjoyed these solemn, tender
thoughts far more than did others, for in the depths of our
heart we both had a strain of sadness, given us by God or
our mother.

Meanwhile my father was attacked by a disease which
brought him to his grave in a short time. He passed away in
my arms, and I learned to know death from the lips of the
very person who had given me life. The impression was profound; it is vivid still. It was the first time that the immortality of the soul was clearly present before my eyes. I could
not believe that this lifeless body was the creator of my
thought; I felt it had to come from some other source, and,
in my religious sorrow, close akin to joy, I hoped one day to
join the spirit of my father.

Another circumstance fixed this lofty idea even more
firmly in my mind. My father's features had taken on a
sublime quality in his coffin. Why should this astonishing
mystery not be an indication of our immortality? Could not
all-knowing death have stamped the secrets of another universe on the brow of its victim? And why could the tomb
not have some great vision of eternity?

Overcome with grief Amelia had withdrawn to the seclusion of a tower from which she could hear the chanting of
the priests in the funeral procession and the death knell
reverberating under the vaults of the Gothic château.

I accompanied my father to his last abode, and the earth

closed over his remains. Eternity and oblivion pressed down on him with all their weight, and that very evening the indifferent passer-by trod over his grave. Aside from his daughter and son, it was already as though he had never existed.

Then I had to leave the family shelter, which my brother had inherited. Amelia and I went to live with some aged relatives.

Pausing before the deceptive paths of life, I considered them one by one, but dared not set out along any of them. Amelia would frequently speak of the joy of the religious life, adding that I was the only bond still holding her to the outside world; and her eyes would fix themselves upon me sadly.

With my heart stirred by these devout talks, I would often make my way toward a monastery close by my new dwelling. Once I was even tempted to retire within its walls forever. Happy are they who reach the end of their travels without ever leaving the harbor and have never, as have I, dragged their barren days out over the face of the earth!

In our endless agitation we Europeans are obliged to erect lonely retreats for ourselves. The greater the turmoil and din in our hearts, the more we are drawn to calmness and silence. These shelters in my country are always open to the sad and weak. Often they are hidden in little valleys, which seem to harbor in their bosom a vague feeling of sorrow and a hope for a future refuge. Sometimes, too, they are found in high places where the religious soul, like some mountain plant, seems to rise toward heaven, offering up its perfumes.

I can still see the majestic mingling of waters and forests around that ancient abbey, where I hoped to shelter my life from the whims of fate; I still wander at eventide in those reverberating, solitary cloisters. When the moon cast its wan light on the pillars of the arcades and outlined their shadow on the opposite wall, I would stop to contemplate the cross marking the burial ground and the tall grass growing among the tombstones. O men who once lived far removed from the world and have passed from the silence of life to the silence of death, how your tombs filled my soul with disgust for this earth!

Whether it was my natural instability or a dislike of the monastic life, I do not know, but I changed my plans and decided to go abroad. As I bade my sister farewell, she clasped me in her arms in an almost joyful gesture, as though she were happy to see me leave, and I could not repress a bitter thought about the inconstancy of human affections.

Nevertheless, I set forth all alone and full of spirit on the stormy ocean of the world, though I knew neither its safe ports nor its perilous reefs. First I visited peoples who exist no more. I went and sat among the ruins of Rome and Greece, those countries of virile and brilliant memory, where palaces are buried in the dust and royal mausoleums hidden beneath the brambles. O power of nature and weakness of man! A blade of grass will pierce through the hardest marble of these tombs, while their weight can never be lifted by all these mighty dead!

Sometimes a tall column rose up solitary in a waste land, as a great thought may spring from a soul ravaged by time and sorrow.

I meditated on these monuments at every hour and through all the incidents of the day. Sometimes, I watched the same sun which had shone down on the foundation of these cities now setting majestically over their ruins; soon afterwards, the moon rose between crumbling funeral urns into a cloudless sky, bathing the tombs in pallid light. Often in the faint, dream-wafting rays of that planet, I thought I saw the Spirit of Memory sitting pensive by my side.

But I grew weary of searching through graveyards, where too often I stirred up only the dust of a crime-ridden past.

I was anxious to see if living races had more virtue and less suffering to offer than those which had vanished. One day, as I was walking in a large city, I passed through a secluded and deserted courtyard behind a palace. There I noticed a statue pointing to a spot made famous by a certain sacrifice. I was struck by the stillness of the surroundings;

only the wind moaned weakly around the tragic marble. Workmen were lying about indifferently at the foot of the statue or whistled as they hewed out stones. I asked them what the monument meant; some knew little indeed, while the others were totally oblivious of the catastrophe it commemorated. Nothing could indicate so vividly the true import of human events and the vanity of our existence. What has become of those figures whose fame was so widespread? Time has taken a step and the face of the earth has been made over.

In my travels I especially sought out artists and those inspired poets whose lyres glorify the gods and the joy of peoples who honor their laws, their religion, and their dead. These singers come of a divine race and possess the only sure power which heaven has granted earth. Their life is at once innocent and sublime. They speak like immortals or little children. They explain the laws of the universe and cannot themselves understand the most elementary concerns of life. They have marvelous intuitions of death and die with no consciousness of it, like new-born infants.

On the mountain peaks of Caledonia, the last bard ever heard in those wildernesses sang me poems which had once consoled a hero in his old age. We were sitting on four stones overgrown with moss; at our feet ran a brook, and in the distance the roebuck strayed among the ruins of a tower, while from the seas the wind whistled in over the waste land of Cona. The Christian faith, itself a daughter of the lofty mountains, has now placed crosses over the monuments of Morven heroes and plucked the harp of David on the banks of the very stream where once the harp of Ossian sighed. Loving peace even as the divinities of Selma loved war, it now shepherds flocks where Fingal once joined battle and has strewn angels of peace amongst clouds once occupied by murderous phantoms.

Ancient, lovely Italy offered me its host of masterworks. With what reverent and poetic awe I wandered through those vast edifices consecrated to religion by the arts! What a labyrinth of columns! What a sequence of arches and vaults! How beautiful are the echoes circling round those domes like the rolling of waves in the ocean, like the murmur of winds in the forest or the voice of God in his temple! The architect seems to build the poet's thoughts and make them accessible to the senses.

And yet with all my effort what had I learned until then? I had discovered nothing stable among the ancients and nothing beautiful among the moderns. The past and present are imperfect statues—one, quite disfigured, drawn from the ruins of the ages, and the other still devoid of its future perfection.

But, my old friends, you who have lived so long in the wilderness, you especially will be surprised that I have not once spoken of the glories of nature in this story of my travels.

One day I climbed to the summit of Etna, that great volcano burning in the middle of an island. Above me, I saw the sun rising in the vast reaches of the horizon, while at my feet Sicily shrank to a point and the sea retreated into the distant spaces. In this vertical view of the picture the rivers seemed little more than lines traced on a map. But while on one side I observed this sight, on the other my eye plunged into the depths of Etna's crater, whose bowels I saw blazing between billows of black smoke.

A young man full of passion, sitting at the mouth of a volcano and weeping over mortal men whose dwellings he could barely distinguish far off below him—O revered elders! Such a creature is doubtless worthy only of your pity! But think what you may, such a picture reveals my character and my whole being. Just so, throughout my life, I have had before my eyes an immense creation which I could barely discern, while a chasm yawned at my side.

As he uttered these last words René grew silent and soon sank into revery. Father Souël looked at him in surprise, while the blind and aged sachem, not hearing the young man's voice any more, did not know what to make of this silence.

René had fixed his eyes on a group of Indians gaily passing through the plain. Suddenly his countenance softened, and tears fell from his eyes.

"Happy Indians," he exclaimed, "oh, why can I not enjoy the peace which always goes with you! While my fruitless wanderings led me through so many lands, you, sitting quietly under your oaks, let the days slip by without counting them. Your needs were your only guide, and, far better than I, you have reached wisdom's goal through your play and your sleep—like children. Your soul may sometimes have been touched by the melancholy of extreme happiness, but you emerged soon enough from this fleeting sadness, and your eyes rose toward heaven, tenderly seeking the mysterious presence which takes pity on the poor Indian."

Here René's voice broke again, and the young man bowed his head. Chactas held his hands out in the shadows, and, touching his son's arm, he exclaimed, deeply moved, "My son! My dear son!" The ring of his voice drew René from his revery, and, blushing at his weakness, he begged his father to forgive him.

Then the aged Indian spoke thus: "My young friend, a heart such as yours cannot be placid; but you must try to temper your character, which has already brought you so much grief. Do not be surprised that you suffer more than others from the experiences of life; a great soul necessarily holds more sorrow than a little one. Go on with your story. You have taken us through part of Europe; now tell us about your own country. As you know, I have seen France and am deeply attached to it. I would like to hear of the great chief who has now passed on, and whose magnificent cabin I once visited. My child, I live only for the past. An old man with his memories is like a decrepit oak in our woods; no longer able to adorn itself with its own foliage, it is obliged to cover its nakedness with foreign plants which have taken root on its ancient boughs."

Calmed by these words, René once more took up the story of his heart.

Alas, father, I cannot tell you about that great century, for I saw only the end of it as a child; it had already drawn to a close when I returned to my land. Never has a more astonishing, nor a more sudden change taken place in a people. From the loftiness of genius, from respect for religion and dignity in manners everything suddenly degenerated to cleverness and godlessness and corruption.

So it had been useless indeed to try to find something in my own country to calm this anxiety, this burning desire which pursues me everywhere. Studying the world had taught me nothing, and yet I had lost the freshness of innocence.

By her strange behavior, my sister seemed bent on increasing my gloom. She had left Paris a few days before my arrival, and when I wrote that I expected to join her, she hastened to dissuade me, claiming she did not know where her business might take her. How sadly I reflected on human affection. It cools in our presence and vanishes in our absence; in adversity it grows weak and in good fortune weaker still.

Soon I found myself lonelier in my native land than I had been on foreign soil. I was tempted to plunge for a time into a totally new environment which I could not understand and which did not understand me. My heart was not yet wasted by any kind of passion, and I sought to find someone to whom I could become attached. But I soon discovered that I was giving more of myself than I was receiving of others. It was neither lofty language nor deep feeling which the world asked of me. I was simply reducing my being to the level of society. Everywhere I was taken for an impractical dreamer. Ashamed of the role I was playing and increasingly repulsed by men and things, I finally decided to retire to some smaller communty where I could live completely by myself.

At first I was happy enough in this secluded, independent life. Unknown by everyone, I could mingle with the crowd—that vast desert of men! Often I would sit in some lonely church, where I could spend hour after hour in meditation. I saw poor women prostrating themselves before the Almighty or sinners kneeling at the seat of penitence. None emerged from this retreat without a more serene expression, and the muffled noises drifting in from outside seemed like waves of passion or storms of the world subsiding at the foot of the Lord's temple. Mighty God, who from Thy solitude couldst see my tears falling in that holy shelter, Thou knowest how many times I threw myself at Thy feet, imploring Thee to relieve me of the weight of my existence or make over the old man within me! Ah, who has never felt a need of regeneration, of growing young in the waters of the spring and refreshing his soul in the fountain of life? Who does not sometimes feel himself crushed by the burden of his own corruption and incapable of anything great or noble or just!

When night had closed in I would start back to my retreat, pausing on the bridges to watch the sunset. As the great star kindled the mists of the city, it seemed to swing slowly in a golden fluid like the pendulum of some clock of the ages. Then I retired with the night through a labyrinth of solitary streets. As I passed lights shining in the dwellings of men, I imagined myself among the scenes of sorrow and joy which they revealed, and I reflected that under all those roofs sheltering so many people, I had not a single friend. In the midst of these thoughts, the hour began tolling in measured cadence from the tower of the Gothic cathedral, and its message was taken up from church to church in a wide range of tones and distances. Alas! Every hour in society lays open a grave and draws fresh tears.

But this life, which at first was so delightful, soon became intolerable. I grew weary of constantly repeating the same scenes and the same thoughts, and I began to search my soul to discover what I really sought. I did not know; but suddenly it occurred to me that I might be happy in the woods. Immediately I resolved to adopt a country exile where I could spend the rest of my days, for, though scarcely begun, my life had already consumed centuries.

I adopted this plan with the ardor typical of all my projects and left at once to retire into seclusion in some rustic cabin, just as previously I had left to travel around the world.

People accuse me of being unpredictable in my tastes, of being unable for long to cherish any single illusion. They consider me the victim of an imagination which plunges toward the end of all pleasures as though it suffered from their duration. They accuse me of forever overreaching the goal I can achieve. Alas! I am only in search of some unknown good, whose intuition pursues me relentlessly. Am I to blame if everywhere I find limitations, if all that is finite I consider worthless? And yet, I feel that I love the monotony in the feelings of life, and, if I were still foolish enough to believe in happiness, I would seek it in an orderly existence.

Total solitude and the spectacle of nature soon brought me to a state almost impossible to describe. Practically bereft of relatives and friends on earth, and never having been in love, I was furiously driven by an excess of life. Sometimes I blushed suddenly and felt torrents of burning lava surging through my heart. Sometimes I would cry out involuntarily, and the night was disturbed both by my dreams and by sleepless cares. I felt I needed something to fill the vast emptiness of my existence. I went down into the valley and up on the mountain, calling, with all the strength of my desire, for the ideal creature of some future passion. I embraced her in the winds and thought I heard her in the river's moaning. Everything became this vision of my imagination—the stars in the skies and the very principle of life in the universe.

Nevertheless, this state of calm and anxiety, of poverty and wealth was not wholly without charm. One day I amused myself by stripping the leaves from a willow branch, one by one, and throwing them into the stream, attaching a thought to each leaf as the current carried it off. A king in fear of losing his crown in a sudden revolution does not feel sharper pangs of anguish than did I, as I watched each peril threatening the remains of my bough. O frailty of mortal man! O childishness of the human heart, which never grows old! How infantile our haughty reason can become! And yet how many men attach their existence to such petty things as my willow leaves!

How can I describe the host of fleeting sensations I felt in my rambles? The echoes of passion in the emptiness of a lonely heart are like the murmurings of wind and water in the silence of the wilderness—they offer their joy, but cannot be portrayed.

Autumn came upon me in the midst of this uncertainty, and I welcomed the stormy months with exhilaration. Sometimes I wished I were one of those warriors who wander amongst winds, clouds, and phantoms, while at other times I was envious even of the shepherd's lot, as I watched him warming his hands by the humble brushwood fire he had built in a corner of the woods. I listened to his melancholy airs and remembered that in every land the natural song of man is sad, even when it renders happiness. Our heart is a defective instrument, a lyre with several chords missing, which forces us to express our joyful moods in notes meant for lamentation.

During the day I roamed the great heath with its forests in the distance. How little I needed to wander off in revery— a dry leaf blown before me by the wind, a cabin with smoke drifting up through the bare tree tops, the moss trembling in the north wind on the trunk of an oak, an isolated rock, or a lonely pond where the withered reed whispered . . . The solitary steeple far off in the valley often drew my attention. Many times, too, my eyes followed birds of passage as they flew overhead. I imagined the unknown shores and distant climes for which they were bound—and how I would have loved to be on their wings! A deep intuition tormented me; I felt that I was no more than a traveler myself, but a voice from heaven seemed to be telling me, "Man, the season for thy migration is not yet come; wait for the wind of death to spring up, then wilt thou spread thy wings and fly toward those unexplored realms for which thy heart longs."

Rise swiftly, coveted storms, coming to bear me off to the spaces of another life! This was my plea, as I plunged ahead with great strides, my face all aflame and the wind whistling through my hair, feeling neither rain nor frost, bewitched, tormented, and virtually possessed by the demon of my heart.

At night, when the fierce wind shook my hut and the rain fell in torrents on my roof, as I looked out through my window and saw the moon furrowing the thick clouds like a pallid vessel ploughing through the waves, it seemed to me that life grew so strong in the depths of my heart that I had the power to create worlds. Ah, if only I could have shared with someone else the delight I felt! O Lord, if only Thou hadst given me a woman after my heart's desire, if Thou hadst drawn from my side an Eve, as Thou didst once for our first father, and brought her to me by the hand . . . Heavenly beauty! I would have knelt down before you, and then, clasping you in my arms, I would have begged the Eternal Being to grant you the rest of my life!

Alas! I was alone, alone in the world! A mysterious apathy gradually took hold of my body. My aversion for life, which I had felt as a child, was returning with renewed intensity. Soon my heart supplied no more nourishment for my thought, and I was aware of my existence only in a deep sense of weariness.

For some time I struggled against my malady, but only halfheartedly, with no firm will to conquer it. Finally, unable to find any cure for this strange wound of my heart, which was nowhere and everywhere, I resolved to give up my life.

Priest of the Almighty, now listening to my story, forgive this poor creature whom Heaven had almost stripped of his reason. I was imbued with faith, and I reasoned like a sinner; my heart loved God, and my mind knew Him not. My actions, my words, my feelings, my thoughts were nothing but contradictions, enigmas, and lies. But does man always know what he wishes, and is he always sure of what he thinks?

Affection, society, and seclusion, everything was slipping away from me at once. I had tried everything, and everything had proved disastrous. Rejected by the world and abandoned by Amelia, what had I left now that solitude had failed me? It was the last support which I had hoped could save me, and now I felt it too giving way and dropping into the abyss!

Having decided to rid myself of life's burden, I now resolved to use the full consciousness of my mind in committing this desperate act. Nothing made it necessary to take action quickly. I did not set a definite time for my death, so that I might savor the final moments of my existence in long, full draughts and gather all my strength, like the men of antiquity, to feel my soul escaping.

I felt obliged, however, to make arrangements about my worldly goods and had to write to Amelia. A few complaints escaped me concerning her neglect, and doubtless I let her sense the tenderness which overcame my heart as I wrote. Nevertheless, I thought I had succeeded in concealing my secret; but my sister was accustomed to reading into the recesses of my heart, and she guessed it at once. She was alarmed at the restrained tone of my letter and at my questions about business matters which had never before concerned me. Instead of answering she came to see me at once with no advance warning.

To realize how bitter my sorrow was later to be and how delighted I was now to see Amelia again, you must understand that she was the only person in the world I had ever loved, and all my feelings converged in her with the sweetness of my childhood memories. And so I welcomed Amelia with a kind of ecstasy in my heart. It had been so long since I had found someone who could understand me and to whom I could reveal my soul!

Throwing herself in my arms, Amelia said to me: "How ungrateful! You want to die and your sister is still alive! You doubt her heart! Don't explain and don't apologize, I know everything; I guessed your intention as though I had been with you. Do you suppose I can be misled, I who watched the first stirrings of your heart? So this is your unhappy character, your dislikes and injustices! Swear to me, while I press you to my heart, swear that this is the last time you will give in to your foolishness; make an oath never to try to take your life again."

As she uttered these words, Amelia looked at me compassionately, tenderly, covering my brow with kisses; she was almost a mother, she was something more tender. Alas! Once again my heart opened out to life's every joy. Like a child, I had only to be consoled, and I quickly surrendered to Amelia's influence. She insisted on a solemn oath, and I readily swore it, not suspecting that I could ever again be unhappy.

Thus we spent more than a month getting used to the delight of being together again. When, instead of finding myself alone in the morning, I heard my sister's voice, I felt a thrill of joy and contentment. Amelia had received some divine attribute from nature. Her soul had the same innocent grace as her body; her feelings were surpassingly gentle, and in her manner there was nothing but softness and a certain dreamy quality. It seemed as though her heart, her thought, and her voice were all sighing in harmony. From her womanly side came her shyness and love, while her purity and melody were angelic.

But the time had come when I was to atone for all my erratic ways. In my madness I had gone so far as to hope some calamity would strike me, so that I might at least have some real reason for suffering—it was a terrible wish, which God in His anger has granted all too well!

O my friends, what am I about to reveal to you! See how these tears flow from my eyes. Can I even . . . Only a few days ago nothing could have torn this secret from me . . . But now, it is all over!

Still, O revered elders, let this story be buried in silence forever; remember that it was meant to be told only under this tree in the wilderness.

Winter was drawing to a close, when I became aware that Amelia was losing her health and repose, even as she was beginning to restore them to me. She was growing thin, her eyes became hollow, her manner listless, and her voice unsteady. People or solitude, my absence or presence, night or day—everything frightened her. Involuntary sighs would die on her lips. Sometimes long distances would not tire her out, and at other times she could barely move about. She would take up her work and set it down, open a book and find it impossible to read, begin a sentence and not finish it, and then she would suddenly burst into tears and go off to pray.

I tried vainly to discover her secret. When I pressed her in my arms and questioned her, she smilingly answered that she was like myself—she did not know what was wrong with her.

Thus three months went by, and each day her state grew worse. The source of her tears seemed to be a mysterious correspondence she was having, for she appeared calmer or more disturbed according to the letters she received. Finally one morning as the time for breakfast had passed, I went up to her rooms. I knocked, but received no answer. I pushed the door ajar; no one was in the room. On the mantel there was an envelope addressed to me. Snatching it up with trembling fingers, I tore it open and read this letter, which will remain with me forever to discourage any possible feeling of joy.

To René:

"My brother, Heaven bears me witness that I would give up my life a thousand times to spare you one moment's grief. But miserable as I am, I can do nothing to make you happy. Forgive me, then, for stealing away from you as though I were guilty. I could never have resisted your pleas, and yet I had to leave. . . . Lord, have pity on me!

"You know, René, that the religious life has always attracted me. Now the time has come to heed Heaven's call. Only why have I waited so long? God is punishing me for it. It was for you alone that I remained in the world . . . But forgive me; I am upset by the sadness of having to leave you.

"Dear brother, it is only now that I feel the full need of those retreats which I have heard you condemn so often. There are certain sorrows which separate us from men forever; were it not for such shelters, what would become of some unfortunate women! . . . I am convinced that you, too, would find rest in these religious havens, for the world has nothing to offer which is worthy of you.

"I shall not remind you of your oath; I know how reliable your word is. You have sworn it, and you will go on living for my sake. Is there anything more pitiful than thinking constantly of suicide? For a man of your character it is easy to die. Believe me, it is far more difficult to live.

"But, my brother, you must give up this solitude at once; it is not good for you. Try to find some kind of occupation. I realize that you bitterly despise the usual necessity of 'becoming established' in France. But you must not scorn all the experience and wisdom of our fathers. Dear René, it is better to resemble ordinary men a little more and be a little less miserable.

"Perhaps you will find relief from your cares in marriage. A wife and children would take up your days. And what woman would not try to make you happy! The ardor of your soul, the beauty of your thought, your noble, passionate air, that proud and tender expression in your eyes, everything would assure you of her love and loyalty. Ah, how joyfully she would clasp you in her arms and press you to her heart! How her eyes and her thoughts would always be fixed on you to shield you from the slightest pain!

In your presence she would become all love and innocence; you would feel that you had found a sister again.

"I am leaving for the convent of B——. It is a cloister built by the edge of the sea and wholly suited to the state of my soul. At night, from within my cell, I shall hear the murmur of the waves as they lap against the convent walls. I shall dream of those walks we once took through the woods, when we fancied we heard the sound of the sea in the tops of the waving pines. Beloved childhood friend, will I ever see you again? Though hardly older than you, I once rocked you in your cradle. Many times we used to sleep together. Ah, if we might one day be together again in the same tomb! But no, I must sleep alone beneath the icy marble of that sanctuary where girls who have never known love rest in eternal peace.

"I do not know whether you will succeed in reading these lines, blurred as they are by my tears. After all, sweet friend, a little sooner or a little later, would we not have had to part? Need I speak of the uncertainty and emptiness of life? You remember young M—— whose ship was lost off the island of Mauritius. When you received his last letter a few months after his death, his earthly remains did not even exist any more, and just when you began to mourn for him in Europe, others in the Indies were ending their mourning. What can man be, then, when his memory perishes so quickly! When some of his friends learn of his death, others are already consoled! Tell me, dear, beloved René, will my memory, too, vanish so quickly from your heart? O my brother, I tear myself away from you in earthly time only that we may not be parted in eternity.

AMELIA

"P.S. I am enclosing the deed of my worldly goods. I hope you will not reject this token of my affection."

Had lightning struck at my feet I could not have been seized by greater panic. What secret was Amelia hiding from me? Who was forcing her into the religious life so suddenly?

And had she reconciled me to life through her tender affection only to abandon me now so abruptly? Oh, why had she come back to turn me aside from my plan? A feeling of pity had brought her back to me, but now, tired of her disagreeable duty, she was impatiently leaving me to my misery, though I had no one but her in all the world. People imagine they have done something wonderful when they have kept a man from death! Such were my sad reflections. Then, examining my own feelings, I said, "Ungrateful Amelia, if you were in my place, if, like myself, you were lost in the void of your existence, ah, you would not be forsaken by your brother!"

And yet, as I reread the letter, I felt in its tone something so sad, so tender, that my heart melted completely. Suddenly I had a thought which gave me hope. It occurred to me that Amelia might have fallen in love with a man, and dared not admit it. This suspicion seemed to explain her melancholy, her mysterious correspondence, and the passionate tone pervading her letter. I wrote to her at once, begging her to open her heart to me. Her answer was not long in coming, but revealed nothing about her secret. She wrote only that she had obtained dispensation from the novitiate and was about to pronounce her vows.

I was exasperated by Amelia's stubbornness, by the enigma of her words, and her lack of confidence in my affection. After hesitating a little about what I would do next, I decided to go to B—— to attempt one last effort to win back my sister. On my way I had to pass through the region where I was brought up. When I caught sight of the woods where I had spent the only happy moments of my life I could not hold back my tears, and I found it impossible to resist the temptation of bidding them a last farewell.

My elder brother had sold the family heritage, and the new owner did not live on the estate. I went up to the château through a long lane of pines. Walking across the deserted courtyard I stopped to gaze at the closed or partly broken windows, the thistle growing at the foot of the walls, the leaves strewn over the threshold of the doors, and that lonely stone stairway where so often I had seen my father and his faithful servants. The steps were already covered with moss, and yellow stock grew between the loose, shaky stones. A new caretaker brusquely opened the doors for me. When I hesitated in crossing the threshold, the fellow exclaimed: "Well, are you going to do what that strange woman did who was here a few days ago? She fainted as she was about to come in, and I had to carry her back to her carriage." It was easy enough for me to recognize the "strange woman" who, like myself, had come back to this spot to find memories and tears!

Drying my eyes with a handkerchief I entered the dwelling of my ancestors. I paced through the resounding halls where nothing could be heard but the beat of my footsteps. The chambers were barely lit by a faint glimmer filtering in through the closed shutters. First I went to see the room where my mother had given her life to bring me into the world, then the room to which my father used to retire, after that the one where I had slept in my cradle, and finally the one where my sister had received my first confessions into the bosom of her love. Everywhere the rooms were neglected, and spiders spun their webs in the abandoned beds. I left the château abruptly and strode quickly away, never daring to turn my head. How sweet, but how fleeting, are those moments spent together by brothers and sisters in their younger years under the wing of their aged parents! The family of man endures but a day, and then God's breath scatters it away like smoke. The son barely knows the father or the father the son, the brother the sister or the sister the brother! The oak sees its acorns take root all around it; it is not so with the children of men!

Arriving at B—— I was taken to the convent, where I asked for an opportunity to speak with my sister. I was told she could not see anybody. I wrote to her, and she replied that, as she was about to be consecrated to God, she was not permitted to turn her thought to the world, and if I loved her, I would avoid burdening her with my sorrow. To this she added: "However, if you plan to appear at the altar on the day of my profession, be pleased to serve as my father. It is the only role worthy of your courage, and the only fitting one for our affection and my peace of mind."

This cold determination resisting my burning affection threw me into a violent rage. There were times when I was about to return where I had come from; then, again, I wanted to stay for the sole purpose of disturbing the sacrifice. Hell even goaded me on with the thought of stabbing myself in the church and mingling my last sighs with the vows tearing my sister away from me. The mother superior of the convent sent word that a bench had been prepared for me in the sanctuary and invited me to attend the ceremony, which was to take place the very next day.

At daybreak I heard the first sound of the bells . . . About ten o'clock I dragged myself to the convent in a deathlike stupor. Nothing can ever again be tragic to a man who has witnessed such a spectacle, nor can anything ever again be painful for one who has lived through it. The church was filled with a huge throng. I was led to the bench in the sanctuary, and immediately I fell on my knees, practically unconscious of where I was or what I intended to do. The priest was already at the altar. Suddenly the mysterious grille swung open and Amelia came forward resplendent in all the finery of the world. So beautiful was she, so divinely radiant her countenance, that she brought a gasp of surprise and admiration from the onlookers. Overcome by the glorious sorrow of her saintly figure and crushed by the grandeur of religion, I saw all my plans of violence crumbling. My strength left me. I felt myself bound by an all-powerful hand, and, instead of blasphemy and threats, I could find in my heart only profound adoration and sighs of humility.

Amelia took her place beneath a canopy, and the sacrifice began by the light of torches amid flowers and aromas which lent their charm to this great renunciation. At the offertory the priest put off all his ornaments, keeping only a linen tunic; then, mounting the pulpit, he described in a simple, moving discourse the joy of the virgin who is consecrated to the Lord. As he pronounced the words, "She appeared like the incense consumed in the fire," deep calm and heavenly fragrances seemed to spread through the audience. It was as if the mystic dove had spread its wings to offer its shelter, while angels seemed to hover over the altar and fly back toward heaven with crowns and perfumes.

Ending his discourse, the priest donned his vestments once more and went on with the sacrifice. Sustained by two young sisters, Amelia knelt down on the bottom step of the altar. Then someone came to get me in order that I might fulfill my role as a father. At the sound of my faltering steps in the sanctuary Amelia was about to collapse. I was placed beside the priest for I was to offer him the scissors. At that moment once again I suddenly felt my passion flame up within me. I was about to burst out in fury, when Amelia recovered her courage and darted such a sad and reproachful glance at me that I was transfixed. Religion was triumphant. Taking advantage of my confusion, Amelia boldly brought her head forward; under the holy blades her magnificent tresses fell in every direction. Her worldly ornaments were replaced by a long muslin robe, which sacrificed none of her appeal. The cares of her brow vanished under a linen headband, and the mysterious veil, that twofold symbol of virginity and religion, was placed on her shorn head. Never had she appeared so beautiful. The penitent's eye was fixed on the dust of the world, while her soul was already in heaven.

However, Amelia had not yet pronounced her vows, and in order to die for the world she had to pass through the tomb. She therefore lay down on the marble slab, and over her was spread a pall, while a torch burned at each of the four corners. With his stole round his neck and his book in his hand, the priest began the service for the dead. The young virgins took it up. O joys of religion, you are powerful indeed, but oh, how terrible! I was obliged to kneel beside this mournful sight. Suddenly a confused murmur emerged from under the shroud, and as I leaned over, my ears were struck by these dreadful words, audible only to myself: "Merciful God, let me never again rise from this deathbed, and may Thy blessings be lavished on my brother, who has never shared my forbidden passion!"

With these words escaping from the bier the horrible truth suddenly grew clear, and I lost control of my senses. Falling across the death sheet I pressed my sister in my arms and cried out: "Chaste spouse of Christ, receive this last embrace through the chill of death and the depths of eternity which already have parted you from your brother!"

This impulse, this cry, and these tears disturbed the ceremony. The priest interrupted himself, the sisters shut the grille, the crowd pushed forward toward the altar, and I was carried away unconscious. Surely I was not grateful to those who revived me! Opening my eyes, I learned that the sacrifice had been consummated, and my sister had been taken with a violent fever. She sent word begging me not to try to see her again. O misery of my life—a sister fearing to talk to her brother, and a brother afraid of having his sister hear his voice! I left the convent as though it were the place of atonement which prepares us in flames for the blessed life, and where all has been lost, as it is in hell—save hope.

There is strength in our soul to sustain us in our own misfortunes, but to become the involuntary cause of someone else's misfortune is completely unbearable. Now that I understood my sister's grief, I imagined how she must have suffered. Several things which I had been unable to understand now became clear—the joy tinged with sadness which my sister had felt when I was leaving on my travels, the efforts she made to avoid me when I had returned, and at the same time, the weakness which kept her from entering a convent for so long. In her sorrow she must have tried to convince herself that she could yet be cured! As for the secret correspondence which had so deceived me—that was apparently made up of her plans to retire from the world and her arrangements for dispensation from the novitiate, as well as the transfer of her property to me.

O my friends, now I knew what it meant to shed tears for grief which was far from imaginary! My emotions, which had been vague for so long, now seized avidly upon this, its first prey. I even felt a kind of unexpected satisfaction in the fullness of my anguish, and I became aware, with a sense of hidden joy, that sorrow is not a feeling which consumes itself like pleasure.

I had wanted to withdraw from the world before receiving the Almighty's command—that was a great crime. God had sent me Amelia both to save and to punish me. Thus does every guilty thought and forbidden act bring on disorder and sorrow. Amelia had begged me to continue living, and I owed it to her not to aggravate her woes. Besides— how strange it seems!—now that my sorrows were real, I no longer wished to die. My grief had become an immediate concern occupying my every moment, so thoroughly is my heart molded of weariness and misery!

And so I suddenly settled on another plan of action; I determined to leave Europe and go to America. At that very time, in the port of B——, they were fitting out a fleet of ships bound for Louisiana. I made arrangements with one of the captains, wrote to Amelia about my plan, and prepared to leave.

My sister had been at the gates of death, but God had reserved for her the supreme crown of virgins and chose not to call her to Him so soon. Her trials on earth were prolonged. Coming down once again into life's painful path she went courageously forward as a heroine in the face of affliction; bent under the cross she saw in her struggles the certainty of triumph and overwhelming glory in her overwhelming woe.

The sale to my brother of what little property I still had, the long preparations of the convoy, and unfavorable winds, all held me in port a long time. Each morning I would go for news of Amelia, and always I returned with new reasons for weeping and admiring.

I wandered endlessly about the convent at the edge of the sea. Often I would notice, in a little grilled window overlooking the deserted beach, a nun sitting in a pensive attitude. She was meditating as she gazed out over the broad ocean, where some vessel could be seen sailing toward the ends of the earth. Several times, in the moonlight, I again saw the nun at the bars of the same window. With the star of night shining down upon her, she was contemplating the sea, listening, it seemed, to the sound of the waves breaking sadly on the lonely shores.

I can still hear the bell in the silence of the night calling the sisters to vigils and prayer. As it tolled in slow rhythm and the virgins moved silently toward the altar of the Almighty, I hastened to the convent. There, alone at the foot of the walls, I would listen in reverent rapture to the last strains of the hymns, as they blended beneath the temple vaults with the gentle murmur of the waves.

I do not know why all these things, which should have intensified my anguish, served instead to soften its sting. My tears were less bitter when I shed them out there on those rocks in the wind. My very grief, which was so rare, bore within itself some remedy; for there is joy in the uncommon, even if it is an uncommon calamity. This almost gave me hope that my sister too might become less miserable.

A letter I received from her before my departure seemed to confirm this feeling. Amelia pitied me tenderly for my sorrow, and assured me that time was healing her wound. "I have not given up hoping for happiness," she wrote. "The very immensity of my sacrifice calms me somewhat, now that it is all over. The simplicity of my companions, the purity of their vows, the regularity of their life, everything spreads its healing balm over my days. When I hear the storms raging and the sea bird beating its wings at my window, I, poor dove of heaven, reflect on my joy in finding a shelter from the tempest. Here is the holy mountain, the lofty summit where we hear the last faint murmurs of the earth and the opening harmonies of heaven. It is here that religion gently beguiles a tender soul. For the most violent passion it substitutes a kind of burning chastity in which lover and virgin are at one. It purifies every sigh, it makes the ephemeral flame inviolate, and it blends its divine calm and innocence with the remains of confusion and worldly joy in a heart seeking rest and a life seeking solitude."

I do not know what heaven still holds in store for me, or whether it meant to warn me that everywhere my steps would be harried by storms. The order was given for our fleet to set sail; as the sun began sinking, several vessels had already weighed anchor. I made arrangements to spend the last night on shore writing my farewell letter to Amelia. Around midnight, as my attention was absorbed in my thoughts and tears moistened my paper, my ear was suddenly drawn to the wailing of the winds. As I listened, cannon shots of alarm could be heard through the storm, together with the knell tolling in the convent. I plunged out to the shore where all was deserted and nothing could be heard but the roar of the surf. I sat down on a rock. On one side I could see the vast expanse of shimmering waves, and on the other the somber walls of the convent vaguely reaching up and fading away in the skies. A dim light shone out from the grilled window. O my Amelia! Was it you, on your knees at the foot of the cross, praying to the God of Tempests to spare your unhappy brother? Storm on the waves, and calm in your retreat; men shattered on the reefs before an unshakeable haven; infinity on the other side of a cell wall; the tossing lights of ships, and the motionless beacon of the convent; the uncertain lot of the seaman, and the vestal's vision in a single day of all the days of her life; and yet, O Amelia, a soul such as yours, stormy as the ocean; a catastrophe more dreadful than the mariner's— this whole picture is still deeply engraved in my memory.

Sun of this new sky, now witness to my tears, echoes of American shores repeating these accents, it was on the morrow of that terrible night that I leaned over the ship's stern and watched my native land disappearing forever! Long I stood there and gazed for the last time at the trees of my country swaying on the shore and the height of the convent sinking over the horizon.

As René came to the end of his story he drew a sheet of paper from his breast and gave it to Father Souël; then, throwing himself into the arms of Chactas and stifling his sobs, he waited as the missionary read through the letter.

It came from the mother superior of B——, and described the last hours in the life of Sister Amelia of Mercy, who had died a victim of her zeal and charity, while caring for companions stricken by a contagious disease. The entire community was inconsolable, and Amelia was regarded as a saint. The mother superior added that in her thirty years as head of the house she had never seen a sister so gentle and calm in disposition and none so happy to be relieved of the world's tribulations.

Chactas clasped René in his arms; the old man was weeping. "My child," he said to his son, "how I wish Father Aubry were here. He could draw from the depths of his heart a strange calm which could pacify storms and yet seemed akin to them. He was the moon on a stormy night. The moving clouds are powerless to carry it along in their flight; pure and unperturbed, it advances serenely above them. Alas, as for me, everything disturbs me and carries me away!"

Until now Father Souël had listened to René's story with a severe countenance and without uttering a word. Although inwardly warm-hearted, he presented to the world an inflexible character. It was the sachem's tenderness which made him break his silence.

"Nothing," he began, "nothing in your story deserves the pity you are now being shown. I see a young man infatuated with illusions, satisfied with nothing, withdrawn from the burdens of society, and wrapped up in idle dreams. A man is not superior, sir, because he sees the world in a dismal light. Only those of limited vision can hate men and life. Look a little farther and you will soon be convinced that all those griefs about which you complain are absolutely nothing. Why, what a shame not to be able to think of the only real misfortune in your life without having to blush! All the purity, all the virtue and faith, and all the crowns of a saint can scarcely make the very idea of your troubles tolerable. Your sister has atoned for her sin, but if I must speak frankly, I fear that through some terrible justice, that confession, emerging from the depths of the tomb, has in turn stirred up your own soul. What do you do all alone in the woods using up your days and neglecting all your duties? You will tell me that saints have retired to the wilderness. Yes, but they were there weeping and subduing their passions, while you seem to be wasting your time inflaming your own. Presumptuous youth, you thought man sufficient unto himself. Know now that solitude is bad for the man who does not live with God. It increases the soul's power while robbing it at the same time of every opportunity to find expression. Whoever has been endowed with talent must devote it to serving his fellow men, for if he does not make use of it, he is first punished by an inner misery, and sooner or later Heaven visits on him a fearful retribution."

Disturbed and humiliated by these words, René raised his head from the bosom of Chactas. The blind sachem began to smile, and this smile of the lips, unrelated as it was to the expression in his eyes, seemed to possess some mysterious, heavenly quality. "My son," said the old man who had once loved Atala, "he speaks severely to both of us; he is reprimanding the old man and the young, and he is right. Yes, you must give up this strange life, which holds nothing but care. Happiness can be found only in the common paths.

"One day the Meschacebe, while yet rather close to its source, grew weary of being only a limpid stream. It called for snows from the mountains, waters from the rivers, and rains from the tempests, and it overran its banks and laid waste its lovely forests. At first the haughty stream applauded its own power. But soon, seeing how everything grew barren along its path and how it now flowed abandoned in its solitude with its waters always troubled, it longed once again for the humble bed which nature had prepared for it, and it pined for the birds and the flowers, the trees and the streams which were once its modest companions along its peaceful course."

Chactas grew silent, and off in the reeds of the Meschacebe the flamingo's call could be heard announcing a storm for the middle of the day. The three friends started back toward their cabins. René walked silently between the missionary, who was praying, and the blind sachem, who kept feeling his way. It is said that, encouraged by the two elders, René returned to his wife, but still found no happiness. Soon afterwards, along with Chactas and Father Souël, he perished in the massacres of the French and Natchez in Louisiana. They still point out a rock where he would go off and sit in the setting sun.

NOTES

Atala

Page 17. *The Floridas, Louisiana.* The term "Floridas" included what is now the state of Florida and a segment of Georgia as well as Alabama, Mississippi, and Louisiana, extending to the Mississippi River. The plural stems from the division of this territory into East Florida, or the peninsula, and West Florida, or the Gulf strip. It was Spanish territory until 1763, when it was ceded to Great Britain. In the same year, also, the immense French possession of "Louisiana" was split, and the part east of the Mississippi was ceded to Great Britain while that west of the Mississippi went to Spain. "Louisiana" was the name loosely applied to the French territory in what is now the United States, and the "vast empire" Chateaubriand mentions here included Canada and Louisiana, extending down to the Floridas, all of which was called New France.

Page 17. *Four great rivers.* In this description Chateaubriand is guided by the hazy and incorrect geographical data of the eighteenth century; the Northwest was as yet unexplored. Carver speaks of these rivers as rising near each other, and identifies the "River of the West" as the Oregon River (now the Columbia River), while the "Bourbon River" is apparently the Nelson River which rises in Lake Winnipeg, into which, in turn, the Winnipeg River empties from the south. An interesting map before the title page in Carver's book, locates these rivers in a vague, fanciful way.

Page 17. *The Meschacebe.* "True name of the Mississippi." (Note of Chateaubriand.) As early as 1832 this picture was already assailed for its inaccuracy and exaggerations. Chateaubriand used as his main sources for his scenery, flora, fauna, and customs, Charlevoix's *Histoire et description générale de la Nouvelle-France* (1744), William Bartram's *Travels through North and South Carolina, Georgia, East and West Florida, the Cherokee Country* (1791), and Jonathan Carver's *Travels through the Interior Parts of North America in the years 1766, 1767 and 1768* (1778; French translation 1784).

Page 17. *The Wabash, the Tenase.* These are actually tributaries not of the Mississippi but of the Ohio.

Page 17. *The hills.* In the French text *montagnes,* mountains.

Page 18. *Pistia.* Tropical duckweed or water lettuce. Sainte-Beuve smiles at such descriptions and observes that "the poet is having a good time," but Bartram writes about these islands as "completely inhabited and alive with crocodiles, serpents, frogs, otters, crows, herons, curlews, jackdaws, etc."

Page 19. *Bears . . . drunk with grapes.* Although Chateaubriand gave page references to his sources, which claim that bears are so partial to grapes that they will climb the highest trees to get them, French critics did not tire of ridiculing this picture. "*The Thousand and One Nights* are a marvel of probability compared with the fable of *Atala*," wrote Abbé de Pradt.

Page 19. *Père Marquette, La Salle, Biloxi, New Orleans.* It was actually De Soto who discovered the Mississippi in the sixteenth century, but Marquette and La Salle, in the following century, were the first to explore it. In the first edition, Chateaubriand had written "Père Hennepin" in place of "Père Marquette." The French settled Biloxi (in what is now the state of Mississippi) in 1699 and New Orleans in 1718.

Page 19. *Natchez.* An Indian tribe occupying the eastern shore of the lower Mississippi, including the spot where the present city of Natchez is located in the state of Mississippi. Here the French built Fort Rosalie (1716). After several quarrels the Natchez attacked the French in 1729, destroyed Fort Rosalie and killed almost all the men. The following year the French and their Indian allies practically annihilated the Natchez. This serves as background for the plight of the Indian band in the Epilogue.

Page 19. *Chactas.* "Harmonious voice." (Note of Chateaubriand.)

Page 20. *Louis XIV, Versailles, Racine, Bossuet.* These represent the high point of French civilization in the seventeenth century. Louis XIV (1643–1715) built the magnificent palace at Versailles which symbolized the glory and power of the "sun king." Racine (1639–1699) is the greatest classical tragedian of France, and Bossuet (1627–1704) its greatest religious orator. Chateaubriand feels obliged to expose Chactas to Western culture, through teachers and travel, in order to make him less primitive and more palatable to French taste.

Page 20. *Antigone, Malvina.* Antigone was the daughter of Oedipus, king of Thebes, and accompanied him into exile after he had blinded himself and been driven out of Thebes for his monstrous, though unwitting, crimes. Mount Cytheron was in Bœotia in ancient Greece. Malvina was the lover of Oscar, son of Ossian, a semilegendary bard and hero of Scotland in the third century, who sang of the exploits of the Caledonians. The skillful imitations of Ossianic poetry by Macpherson in the eighteenth century had a tremendous success and influence in the early nineteenth century and are often alluded to in writings of the French romantics. Morven was a kingdom of ancient Scotland. References such as these, as well as certain stylistic features of *Atala*, help to give it a certain epic flavor.

Page 20. *Fénelon* (1651–1715), archbishop, essayist, and preceptor of the grandson of Louis XIV; Fénelon indoctrinated his pupil with indirect criticisms of his grandfather's failings as a king.

Page 20. *1725.* Chactas is almost 73 years old when he relates his tragedy. When the story begins he is a youth of seventeen; this was, therefore, in 1669. He then spends two and a half years in Saint-Augustine, so that the main drama takes place about 1672. The romantic temper of Chactas and Atala at this date is, of course, an anachronism.

Page 20. *Sachems.* "Elders or Counselors." (Note of Chateaubriand.)

Page 20. *Medicine men.* Chateaubriand's word is *jongleurs,* jugglers or conjurors. Carver describes them as men invested with the triple character of doctor, priest, and magician, able not only to heal diseases but to interpret dreams, give protective charms, predict the future, and commune with the spirits.

Page 20. *Manitous.* Spirits, conceived as having human attributes, though endowed with a nature superior to that of man.

Page 22. *Moon of flowers.* "Month of May." (Note of Chateaubriand.)

Page 22. *Snows.* "Snow for year; seventy-three years." (Note of Chateaubriand.)

Page 22. *Areskoui.* "God of War." (Note of Chateaubriand.)

Page 22. *The land of souls.* "The underworld." (Note of Chateaubriand.)

Page 22. *Saint Augustine . . . newly built.* It was really settled in 1565, but was burned and rebuilt twice, the second burning occurring in 1665 or four years before the arrival of Chactas.

Page 23. *Sadly watching it flow by.* This romantic pastime and the revery of Chactas recall similar activities of Werther in Goethe's *Sorrows of Werther* (May 9).

Page 23. *For I too have sweet memories of it.* Chateaubriand shows the consoling and pacifying value of civilization and religion on Lopez as well as the aged Chactas and Aubry, but he attributes to each of these characters a passionate past.

Page 25. *Corn pudding.* The text has *sagamité* with the footnote "kind of corn mush."

Page 25. *Maiden of Last Love.* According to one of Chateaubriand's sources, Charlevoix, prisoners of war about to be put to death were often well treated among the Huron and Iroquois Indians, and were sometimes even given girls to console their last days.

Page 26. *When the dayfly appears,* i.e., in the spring.

Page 26. *Alachua savannah.* In the northern part of Florida. There is a town in Florida today called Alachua, northwest of Gainesville.

Page 26. *Liquidambar.* Another term for the copalm.

Page 27. *Do children of the cabin.* An echo of Rousseau. It will be noted in the latter part of the work that the hermit has been careful not to take the Indians "too far" along the path of civilization, while, on the other hand, Chactas and Chateaubriand have almost unreserved admiration for the Seminoles, who are of course uninfluenced by European culture.

Page 30. *Shells.* The text has *porcelaines* with the footnote "kind of shell."

Page 30. *So sang the young man.* A fine example of Chateaubriand's talent for transfiguring his sources. The song itself is his own (though it recalls the *Song of Solomon*), but the idea of the lover stealing through the night to find his lady is in Carver, pp. 375–378, where the torch is merely a splinter lighted at the fire of the girl's tent, and the general atmosphere is, to say the least, far less august.

Page 31. *Happy are they who die in the cradle.* Sentiments such as these, as well as the plight of the Indians in the Epilogue, show Chateaubriand's native gloom emerging to color even the theme of the natural man. When placed beside the passages revealing a sentimental and idealized conception of the Indian, seen as a happy, childlike creature, these despondent moments add an element of confusion to the author's general inspiration.

Page 32. *Apalachucla, Chattahoochee.* A town and river in what is now Georgia.

Page 32. *Chichicoué.* "Musical instrument of the savages" (Note of Chateaubriand); a rattle made of a gourd.

Page 33. *Tomahawk.* "Hatchet." (Note of Chateaubriand.)

Page 34. *Ceremony for the Dead.* Performed every eight or ten years, according to Charlevoix.

Page 35. *Blushed.* "Blushing is noticeable among young savages." (Note of Chateaubriand.)

Page 35. *Great Hare.* One of the most potent Indian spirits.

Page 38. *Fire water.* "Brandy." (Note of Chateaubriand.)

Page 39. *Fixed star.* "The North." (Note of Chateaubriand.)

Page 39. *Mocassins.* "Indian footwear." (Note of Chateaubriand.)

Page 40. *Rock-tripe.* Kind of moss growing on rocks, really found only in high northern latitudes.

Page 41. *Sticoe, Keowe.* Chateaubriand seems to follow Bartram, pp. 343, 352–353, for these.

Page 43. *Moon of fire.* "Month of July." (Note of Chateaubriand.)

Page 43. *A thunderstorm.* Chateaubriand's storm is clearly influenced by a single page of Bartram, p. 341, which also describes the darkness, the black clouds, the ominous stillness followed by the din, the birds retiring, the fierce wind, the bending of the forest, and the trembling of the earth; the single word "smoking" may even have given him the idea of the forest fire. Bartram is a real writer as well as an explorer, and his account, while less dramatic, does not yield the palm to Chateaubriand's.

Page 44. *Little tigers.* Bartram observes that what is called "panther" in the northern states is called "tyger" in the southern states.

Page 45. *Cast water in her face.* The worst punishment for Indian children, according to Charlevoix.

Page 45. *Cut off your nose.* Carver, p. 375, says that among the Naudowessies, the husband bites off the nose of an adulterous wife before divorcing her, and Carver actually witnessed one such instance.

Page 46. *A device contrived to deceive us.* This is pronounced by the native pessimist in Chateaubriand, who instinctively feels that the world is set against him.

Page 46–47. *Oh, the surprise.* This point may be likened to the turning point in Wagner's *Tannhäuser* Overture, where the wild and passionate bacchanal slowly gives way before the powerful and beautiful religious theme.

Page 53. *Hallowed ... with a cross.* "Father Aubry had done as the Jesuits in China, who permitted the Chinese to bury their relatives in their gardens, according to their ancient custom." (Note of Chateaubriand.)

Page 54. *For I felt Him descend in my heart.* An example of Rousseauistic deism, the proof of God's existence coming through the heart.

Page 56. *Like the nameless rivers.* This comparison of a life to an obscure stream is taken up by Lamartine in his poem *The Valley (Le Vallon).*

Page 61. *My life at your feet ... in some unknown corner.* The same feeling, previously expressed by Chactas (p. 56), is repeated in Byron's *Childe Harold's Pilgrimage* IV, 177.

> Oh! that the Desert were my dwelling-place,
> With one fair Spirit for my minister,
> That I might all forget the human race,
> And, hating no one, love but only her!

Page 64. *Its rays ... on my grave.* This recalls the loving forethought which the author himself lavished on arrangements for his own impressive tomb. Werther had similarly pictured his own grave in the setting sun (December 21).

Page 66. *Rachel would not be consoled.* Paraphrase of *Jeremiah* XXXI, 15 and *Matthew* II, 18.

Page 67. *Even in the hearts of our friends.* Werther had written almost identically: "Yes, such is the frailty of man, that ... even in the memory, in the heart of his beloved, there also he must perish—vanish—and that quickly." (October 26.)

Page 67. *The old man's calm words.* Chateaubriand writes that his friend Fontanes had disapproved of the original version of this long monologue. The author had returned home disheartened and was unable to write a word. Then, at midnight, suddenly inspired, he composed the new version all at once, without a single change. The next morning he took it to Fontanes, who applauded enthusiastically.

Page 70. *The trace my tears have left upon it.* The crucifix associated with the death of a loved one, borne in the bosom of the man and etched away by his tears, reappears in Lamartine's poem *The Crucifix*.

Page 71. *Condemned to live.* In his *Memoirs* Chateaubriand similarly wrote: "My mother inflicted life on me."

Page 72. *Dazzling white cheeks.* This detail, as well as the "golden tresses" further on, seems strange in the daughter of a Spanish father and an Indian mother. Chateaubriand is doubtless thinking of one of his feminine acquaintances whose memory may have influenced his portrait of Atala. (André Gavoty uses these physical details as well as other moral ones to attempt to identify the model of Atala as Madame de Belloy—see *La Revue*, May 1 and 15, June 1 and 15, 1948. Others have spoken of the young Englishwoman Charlotte Ives. Probably no single woman Chateaubriand knew can account for all of Atala's traits.)

Page 73. *I have passed away like a flower. . . . Wherefore is light given.* The first part is apparently based on such verses as *Job* XIV, 2, *Psalms* CII, 11, and *Psalms* CIII, 15; the second part is from *Job* III, 20.

Page 75. *The heart most serene.* Byron writes similarly:

> Smile on—nor venture to unmask
> Man's heart, and view the Hell that's there.

Childe Harold's Pilgrimage, "To Inez" after I, 84.

Page 76. *Agannonsioni.* "The Iroquois." (Note of Chateaubriand.) It means "cabin builders," because they built cabins more solidly than other Indians.

Page 77. *Apios.* The wild bean or ground nut.

Page 77. *I have seen you.* Actually Chateaubriand visited Italy only after he had published *Atala.*

Page 78. *Esquine water.* China root water.

Page 78. *Its perpendicular height.* Chateaubriand's figure is a little lower than the real height, i.e. 158 feet for the Canadian or Horseshoe Falls and 167 feet for the American Falls.

René

Page 85. *Fort Rosalie.* "French colony at Natchez." (Note of Chateaubriand.) See note to *Atala*, p. 19 (under *Natchez*).

Page 85. *Thus several years went by.* Chactas told his story in 1725; René was killed in the attack by the French in 1730; René therefore tells his story between 1728 and 1730.

Page 86. *The source of his torments within himself.* It was not otherwise that Werther had written (November 3): "I am alone the cause of my own woe.... My own bosom contains the source of all my sorrow."

Page 87. *I cost my mother her life.* This is undoubtedly a reminiscence of the beginning of Rousseau's *Confessions;* Chateaubriand's mother in reality died in 1798 when he was thirty. This paragraph nevertheless is related to the author's life. He tells us in his *Memoirs* that he was born extremely frail, "almost dead," to use his own words. He was immediately entrusted to a nurse at Plancoët, where he remained for three years. "As I emerged from my mother's womb, I was subjected to my first exile.... I hadn't lived more than a few hours when the weight of time was already marked on my brow. Why was I not permitted to die?"

Page 87. *Drawn from the womb with an instrument.* Ostensibly a symbol for the author's protest against life. Atala similarly comes to the world with great pain. René's sadness seems to antedate not only all specific causes of suffering but also existence itself.

Page 87. *I was timid and inhibited.* These paragraphs are based on the author's childhood and adolescence. Curiously enough the hero of Constant's *Adolphe* (1816) also begins by saying: "I found in my father ... a cold and caustic observer."

Page 87. *I courted the Muses.* Chateaubriand wrote verses in his youth before finding his true style in poetic prose.

Page 87. *The sound of the distant bell.* The music of bells recurs in *René* and other works of Chateaubriand. It also is prominent in early romantic English literature which was familiar to Chateaubriand. In 1796 the ringing of bells had been forbidden in France, but the law was generally ignored in country districts.

Page 89. *Amelia ... the religious life.* Lucile was in fact pious and even mystical. At seventeen she regretted the loss of her younger years, read pious texts, and wished to enter a convent.

Page 89. *The burial ground.* These meditations in a cemetery, as well as the solitary walks in nature, particularly in the evening, are reminiscent of such poets as Gray, Thomson and Young. Chateaubriand wrote an article on Young and translated Gray's *Elegy.*

Page 90. *The ruins of Rome and Greece.* Such passages not only made poetry of the ruins popular, but the pilgrimage to Italy, Greece, and the Orient, or variations of this route, became a necessity for writers of the following generation. Chateaubriand's own pilgrimage came after the publication of *René.*

Page 90. *A statue.* "At London, behind Whitehall, the statue of Charles II." (Note of Chateaubriand.) He was apparently deeply affected by this statue, and has written about it elsewhere, adding that Charles II is pointing to the spot where his father Charles I was executed. In reality, it was a bronze statue of James II, the brother of Charles II.

Page 91. *Caledonia, Cona, Morven, Selma, Fingal.* Names in the poetry of Ossian. Caledonia is the poetic name of Scotland; Cona, Morven, and Selma are referred to as places in Scotland; Fingal was Ossian's father. The "four stones overgrown with moss," the "brook," the "roebuck," and the "wind whistling in over the waste land of Cona" are also in Ossian.

Page 93. *"Happy Indians."* An example of the Rousseauistic tendency to idealize the primitive man. The conclusion of the paragraph is influenced by Rousseauistic deism rather than Catholicism.

Page 93. *The great chief . . . magnificent cabin.* "Louis XIV." (Note of Chateaubriand.) Versailles. The naïveté seems a little forced in such an experienced figure as Chactas.

Page 95. *The old man.* A biblical expression, *Ephesians* IV, 22 ("the old man, which is corrupt") and *Colossians* III, 9.

Page 95. *The hour began tolling.* A scene again reminiscent of Gray's *Elegy.*

Page 96. *My life had already consumed centuries.* Chateaubriand precedes a long line of writers in the nineteenth century who were to experience this same feeling of old age in their youth. At the age of twenty-five Flaubert wrote (December 20, 1846): "Under my youthful covering lies a strange old age." In his *Rockets* (*Fusées*) Baudelaire observes: "They say I am thirty years old; but if I have lived three minutes in one, am I not ninety?" Vigny, too, notes in his *Journal of a Poet* when he was twenty-seven, "my life is two hundred years old." And in Italy the desperately sad Leopardi writes in *The Dream* (*Il Sogno*):

> Young am I, yet my youth is all consumed
> And blighted like old age.

Page 96. *Plunges toward the end of all pleasures.* Chateaubriand is the immediate progenitor of Flaubert in this dissatisfaction with all experience. "I like to wear things out," he writes. "I have never had a feeling which I haven't tried to end. When I am in one place, I attempt to be in another. When I see a goal of any kind, I plunge headlong toward it. When I get there, I yawn." (December 31, 1851.)

Page 96. *The ideal creature.* In his *Memoirs* Chateaubriand writes about the "sylph" he dreamed of in his youth; she was an ideal woman composed of the finest features of women he had encountered in his readings, in pictures, in real life, or in his imagination.

Page 97. *Autumn came upon me.* Chateaubriand elaborates his sympathy for the autumn in his *Memoirs.* "The sadder the season, the closer I felt to it." It was in the wake of English poetry that Chateaubriand and his followers began to see autumn not as a joyous season of plenty—as had the classics—but as a season of poignant melancholy.

Page 97. *Warriors who wander.* An Ossianic allusion.

Page 97. *The shepherd's lot* recalls Gray. An example of René's ambivalent attitude: the aspiration to something superior to life on the one hand, and the desire for the pleasures of life on the other.

Page 98. *I was no more than a traveler.* This feeling that the earth is a place of exile was soon to become common among the romantics. Lamartine, for instance, expresses it in *Solitude (L'Isolement)* and *God (Dieu)*.

Page 98. *Alas! I was alone.* This paragraph is a concise rendition of the romantic malady, the French "mal du siècle" or "ennui." Byron describes it as "that settled ceaseless gloom ... That will not look beyond the tomb, But cannot hope for rest before."

Page 98. *I resolved to give up my life.* Chateaubriand tells us that he had tried to take his life in his youth, but the gun failed to go off. "I assumed that my time had not yet come, and I postponed putting my plan into effect until another day."

Page 99. *The final moments of my existence.* Werther had gone about his suicide with this same deliberate calmness.

Page 102. *The world has nothing ... worthy of you.* Similarly Atala at first rejoices in the unfortunate situation her mother has created because she sees all about her only unworthy people. In his *Memoirs* Chateaubriand writes: "A hidden instinct warned me that, as I went forth in the world, I would find nothing I sought."

Page 102. *Better to resemble ordinary men.* The author says of himself in the *Memoirs:* "Had I been more like other men, I should have been happier. If, without robbing me of my intelligence, someone had succeeded in killing my so-called talent, he would have treated me as a friend." Werther, too, laments: "Gracious Providence ... why didst thou not withhold some of those blessings I possess, and substitute in their place a feeling of self-confidence and contentment?" (October 20.)

Page 104. *A last farewell.* This is based on an actual visit of Chateaubriand to Combourg; he saw the old château again in 1791 before leaving for America, and once more around 1801, before publishing *René.* At this latter date the Revolution had already occurred, and this may explain the abandoned condition of the château.

Page 106. *So beautiful was she ... flowers and aromas.* When Chateaubriand was twelve years old, he had witnessed a cousin of his taking the veil. This probably left a deep impression on him.

Page 109. *Satisfaction in the fullness of my anguish.* Expressions such as these (cf. "cherished melancholy" and "sorrow close akin to joy") are too significant to be mere literary paradoxes; in the *Memoirs*, too, Chateaubriand speaks of "this sadness which has been my torment and my felicity."

Page 113. *Why, what a shame.* The same type of reproval concludes *Adolphe:* "I hate that type of vanity which is concerned with itself while telling of the harm it has done, which means to draw pity by describing itself, and which, hovering invulnerable amidst the ruins, analyzes itself instead of repenting."

Page 114. *A rock ... in the setting sun.* This last evocative picture again represents one of the author's personal postures. In the *Memoirs* he writes: "North of the château stretched a plain strewn with druidic rocks; I would go off and sit on one of these in the setting sun. The gilded summit of the woods, the splendor of the earth and the evening star twinkling through the pink clouds brought me back to my dreams ..."